Lutheran Identity
and Mission

WILLIAM H. LAZARETH
PÉRI RASOLONDRAIBE

LUTHERAN IDENTITY AND MISSION

Evangelical and
Evangelistic?

Foreword by Phyllis Anderson

FORTRESS PRESS   Minneapolis

LUTHERAN IDENTITY AND MISSION
Evangelical and Evangelistic?

Cover design: Pollock Design Group

Library of Congress Cataloging-in-Publication data available

ISBN 0-8006-2837-3

Manufactured in the U.S.A.   AF 1–2837

98   97   96   95   94   1   2   3   4   5   6   7   8   9   10

CONTENTS

FOREWORD

THIS VOLUME BRINGS TOGETHER TWO DISTINCT PERSPECTIVES on a single topic: the relationship between Lutheran identity and mission. The Lutheran Confessions of the sixteenth century define the center and establish the boundaries for Lutheran evangelical theology. They have served to defend the radical freedom of the gospel of salvation in Jesus Christ through faith alone. It is much less clear how the Confessions contribute to mission.

Does the Confessional heritage that grounds Lutheran identity in the gospel also provide the basis for a robust Lutheran witness to the gospel in the contemporary world? Do the Confessions function as a corrective to evangelistic excess? Are there aspects of Lutheran Confessional identity that work against mission? Is there anything Christians can do or should do to enhance the effectiveness of their proclamation of the gospel? Or do our efforts compromise God's sovereign freedom? How do we resolve the internal tension within Lutheranism that seems to set evangelicalism and evangelism at odds?

These were the questions identified by the planners of the 1993 Hein/Fry Lecture Series under the theme, "Lutheranism: Evangelical and Evangelistic?" They are questions facing the newly formed Evangelical Lutheran Church in America (ELCA) as it seeks to define its own identity as both solidly evangelical and radically open to service and mission among the many cultures and increasingly unchurched people in America and beyond.

Two prominent theologians were invited to address this topic, each at four of the eight seminaries of the ELCA. They came at the issue from quite different angles and experiences. Their two perspectives, brought together in this volume, help to elucidate, though not necessarily resolve, some of the fundamental tensions that divide Confessional Lutherans on the issue of mission.

Dr. William H. Lazareth is a widely recognized leader and scholar both within his own Lutheran denomination and in the international ecumenical community. He was educated at Princeton University, the Lutheran Seminary at Philadelphia, and Columbia University-Union Theological Seminary. He retired, in 1992, as Bishop of the Metropolitan New York Synod, Evangelical Lutheran Church in America. He has also served as pastor of Holy Trinity Lutheran Church in Manhattan, as Director of the Faith and Order Secretariat of the World Council of Churches in Geneva, and as director of the Department for Church in Society of the former Lutheran Church in America. From 1956 to 1976, Dr. Lazareth was Hagen Professor of Systematic Theology and Dean of Faculty at the Lutheran Theological Seminary at Philadelphia.

While his wide-ranging career has involved him in every aspect of denominational and ecumenical life, Lazareth approaches the topic primarily as a Confessional theologian, without specific reference to his pastoral experience or his North American context. His source is the Lutheran Confessional writings, chiefly Luther's Large Catechism. Following the structure of the catechism, he uses each part in turn to make critical distinctions that define an understanding of mission that is at once confessional, evangelical, and catholic.

Luther's writings on the Ten Commandments, for example, while not related explicitly to mission, do introduce the doctrine of the two kingdoms which defines for Lazareth an evangelical approach to nonbelievers. Evangelism, as a specifically and exclusively Christian activity, is to be sharply distinguished from participation in God's mission to bring peace and justice on earth, which he holds to be inclusive of all people regardless of faith. His primary concern is about the possible confusion between the two. He evidences less concern about the widespread lack of zeal for either mission or evangelism.

Lazareth draws on the articles on the Creed, the Lord's Prayer, and the Sacraments for his understanding of the church as the sacramental sign and instrument in God's plan of salvation. The church does not have a mission. Rather, the church is itself God's mission, God's body sent into the world. Contemporary Lutherans, therefore, should intensify the cultivation of a churchly or communal style of evangelism.

Lazareth is not a critic of the Confessions, but an adept interpreter and unqualified advocate for their usefulness and relevance as theological norm. "The crying need for Lutheran Confessional norms now emerges in bold relief, if our church is to remain truly evangelical while becoming more evangelistic."

Dr. Péri Rasolondraibe explicitly defines his perspective, "not as a professor of confessions or of missions, . . . but as a parish pastor trying to proclaim the good news of Jesus Christ through teaching and apostolic actions in an increasingly secularized and secularizing world." As an evangelical apologist, he works from a Confessional base, but his interest is less in the text itself than in how the text furthers or hinders Christ's call to proclaim the good news.

Dr. Rasolondraibe presently serves as pastor of the four thousand member Ambatovinaky Lutheran Congregation in Antananarivo, the capital of Madagascar. This 120-year-old congregation is the oldest Lutheran parish in Madagascar. It is part of the 840,000-member, 106-year-old Malagasy Lutheran Church, which traces its roots to Norwegian missionary efforts. The Ambatovinaky congregation represents the Malagasy Lutheran Church to governmental and ecumenical bodies in the capital city.

Dr. Rasolondraibe brings broad international experience with both academic theology and practical church life in North America as well as Africa. He holds a Ph.D. from Princeton Theological Seminary. He taught systematic theology for four years at Luther Northwestern Seminary in St. Paul, where he had previously earned his Th.M. degree. He also taught at the Lutheran Theological Seminary in Madagascar, where he served as President from 1984 to 1987.

While Dr. Rasolondraibe is firmly grounded in Lutheran Confessional theology, he brings challenging questions to it from his pastoral experience and from his African context. He reflects on ways in which "sola gratia" is hard to hear and believe in a market-driven, power-oriented global culture, especially for Christians who come from the "project-submitting and scholarship-begging churches." He argues for an understanding of "grace alone" that not only proclaims the good news, but also brings about the good news wherever the church is.

He seizes on the Confessional theme of "sola scriptura" as the key to vital evangelization. The Confessions, responding to the spirit and challenges of their own age, have little to say about sharing the gospel with unbelievers. But they point us to the Scriptures, "sola scriptura." It is emersion in the Scriptures, Rasolondraibe contends, that nurtures evangelical outreach.

Finally, he identifies justification by faith alone, "sola fide," as the starting point that enables evangelical witness in word and deed. "Sola fide" is not faith in the abstract but faith in the Son. It is what he calls the way of "filiation." Following Christ means walking the way of the Son in acts of empowerment for the sake of the weak and the impoverished of the land.

Both Lazareth and Rasolondraibe acknowledge that evangelism, that is, proclaiming the faith to people of other living religions or of no faith at all, was not on the agenda of the reformers. The Confessional writings have very little to say specifically about mission. That absence, however, does not prevent either Lazareth or Rasolondraibe from drawing provocative conclusions about contemporary Christian mission from the gospel, as the reformers understood it and explicated it in the Confessional writings. These essays are works of constructive theology, building new frameworks of understanding that go beyond the historical documents.

These lectures were prepared and delivered by the two authors independently and simultaneously. Because print medium is linear and requires that one thing come before another, the publishers had to decide whose essays should come first in this volume: Lazareth's or Rasolondraibe's. The order does make a difference in the reading. As they stand, Lazareth's work lays down the classical norms for an evangelical understanding of mission as the foundation. Against this background, Rasolondraibe offers challenges out of his own context and creative theological moves that attempt to bridge the gap between the classical, Western norms and the realities of contemporary mission. Had the Rasolondraibe essays come first, Lazareth's careful textual analysis would have served to bring the reader back to an awareness of the dangers involved in all our attempts to adapt the tradition to meet the needs of contemporary culture.

As the reader, you are free to read these lectures in whatever order you choose. But do read them both. Try to resist the temptation to read only the author who confirms your own predisposition. If you succeed, you will be rewarded with a deeper appreciation of what is at stake in the contemporary global struggle to shape a Lutheran identity that serves both the gospel and those who need to hear its saving word.

The Hein/Fry Lecture Series is a program of the Division for Ministry of the Evangelical Lutheran Church in America, supported through the combined endowments honoring preeminent ecclesiastical leaders in antecedent church bodies: Carl Christian Hein, Franklin Clark Fry, Frederick H. Knubel, E. Clarence Miller, Walton S. Greever, and Hilda Drewes Fry.

REV. DR. PHYLLIS ANDERSON
DIRECTOR FOR THEOLOGICAL EDUCATION
DIVISION FOR MINISTRY
EVANGELICAL LUTHERAN CHURCH IN AMERICA

PART I

Lutheranism: Confessional, Evangelical, and Catholic

by William H. Lazareth

CHAPTER 1

Confessional

On April 9, 1945, Lutheran pastor and theologian Dietrich Bonhoeffer was hanged at Flossenbürg Prison in Germany. Only the day before, he had officiated at a Sunday liturgy for his fellow prisoners. The next day he was killed by special order of Heinrich Himmler. The exact date of his execution had been carefully chosen by his Nazi captors. Though it turned out to be only a month before the end of World War II in Europe, April 9 also marked the first anniversary of the unsuccessful attempt involving Bonhoeffer to assassinate the Nazi fuehrer, Adolf Hitler. Today the Lutheran Church annually sets aside April 9 in its liturgical calendar (which fell fittingly on Good Friday in 1993). We praise God for empowering Bonhoeffer's courageous embodiment of the *Cost of Discipleship,* also the later title of one of his most moving books.

Dietrich Bonhoeffer had been an early and prominent leader in the Nazi resistance movement called the "Confessing Church" (*Bekennende Kirche*), centering his protests against the regime's ruthless persecution of the Jews and suppression of the Word of God. During a period of grueling self-examination, Bonhoeffer made a poetic entry in his prison diary that serves well to set both the tone and the direction for our own Lutheran quest today for corporate renewal in mission and evangelism:

"Who Am I?"

Who am I? They often tell me
I would step from my cell's confinement
calmly, cheerfully, firmly,
like a squire from his country-house.

Who am I? They often tell me
I would talk to my warders
freely and friendly and clearly,
as though it were mine to command.

Who am I? They also tell me
I would bear the days of misfortune
equably, smilingly, proudly,
like one accustomed to win.

Am I then really all that which other men tell of?
Or am I only what I know of myself,
restless and longing and sick, like a bird in a cage,
struggling for breath, as though hands were compressing
    my throat,
yearning for colours, for flowers, for the voices of birds,
thirsting for words of kindness, for neighbourliness,
tossing in expectation of great events,
powerlessly trembling for friends at an infinite distance,
weary and empty at praying, at thinking, at making,
faint, and ready to say farewell to it all?

Who am I? This or the other?
Am I one person today and tomorrow another?
Am I both at once? A hypocrite before others,
and before myself a contemptibly woebegone weakling?
Or is something within me still like a beaten army,
fleeing in disorder from victory already achieved?

Who am I? They mock me, these lonely questions of mine.
Whoever I am, thou knowest, O God, I am thine![1]

---

[1]Dietrich Bonhoeffer, *Letters and Papers from Prison* (New York: Macmillan, 1953), pp. 221-22.

In, with, and under painful ambivalence with regard to his historical identification, Bonhoeffer was also confidently certain of his eternal identity: a faithful Christian who belonged to God because of his baptismal incorporation into the death and resurrection of Jesus Christ, within the one holy, catholic, and apostolic church of its Savior and Lord.

"We Believe, Teach, and Confess . . ."

IN A SIMILAR TENSION BETWEEN *THIS* DENOMINATIONAL CHURCH and *the* universal church, much the same could be said of current American Lutheran*ism,* whether as an ecclesiastical "Ism" (which the Lutheran confessors institutionally never sought), or as an ecclesiological "Ism" (which the Lutheran confessors doctrinally never taught). Their "Conservative Reformation" (Charles P. Krauth) was intentionally pursued as an evangelical corrective to late medieval aberrations. As a loyal part of the Western church, they acted in fidelity to God by their apostolic continuity in the gospel. Theirs was truly the apostolic tradition: not the dead faith of the living, but rather the living faith of the dead (Jaroslav Pelikan).

I have elsewhere outlined my understanding of the confessors' catholic intent and evangelical content within the Augsburg Confession, concentrating my work there especially on the doctrine of the office of the ordained ministry.[2] Let me simply reiterate here my basic agreement with the central thesis of Erich Gritsch and Robert Jenson about the authentic genesis of so-called Lutheranism in the sixteenth century:

> As it is, Lutheranism is a confessional movement within the church catholic that continues to offer to the whole church that proposal of dogma which received definitive documentary form in the Augsburg Confession and the

---

[2]William H. Lazareth, *Two Forms of Ordained Ministry: A Proposal for Mission in Light of the Augsburg Confession* (Minneapolis: Augsburg, 1991).

other writings collected in the Book of Concord. . . . The Lutheran proposal of dogma has one great theme: justification by faith alone, apart from works of the law.[3]

To say it as sharply as possible, the Lutheran Confessions aim to keep catholics evangelical and evangelicals catholic. They offer the rest of the whole church an all-decisive soteriological dogma (or doctrine) to fulfill the early church's trinitarian and christological affirmations of faith, which are to be found in the ecumenical councils and creeds. The saving work of God in "Jesus Christ and him crucified" (1 Cor. 2:2) is not merely the theological opinion or devotional piety of one church party. It is rather that all-determinative doctrinal norm of the church catholic — the "north" of its Confessional compass — which is meant to box the rest of all that the body of Christ says and does.

Consequently, I will contend that Lutheranism's unalterable "fingerprint" is its *evangelical catholic confessionality:* "We believe, teach and confess in fidelity to the Word of God." Solely to reenforce the catholic orthodoxy of all creedal Christians, Lutherans characteristically witness to the evangelical doctrine of justification by grace through faith for Christ's sake alone (or one of its other New Testament equivalents) as the normative key for proclaiming the saving work of the triune God, Father, Son, and Holy Spirit.

We learn from church history that it is simply not enough for Christ-centered orthodoxy that Christians be theological or even scriptural. Indeed, most of the notorious heretics and apostates have been both scriptural and theological, however unevangelical and anticatholic. Therefore, in seeking to restore the simultaneous Confessional and ecumenical integrity of Lutheranism, George Lindbeck's *The Nature of Doctrine* is keen to emphasize the crucial distinction between church

---

[3]Eric W. Gritsch and Robert W. Jenson, *Lutheranism: The Theological Movement and Its Confessional Writings* (Philadelphia: Fortress, 1976), p. 6.

doctrine and personal theology, i.e., between communal confessions and individual opinions.[4] In a religious age preoccupied with sectarian "slang," Lindbeck compares and commends the church's doctrine (dogma, creeds, or confessions) to a textbook containing rules and examples of communally accepted (that is, orthodox) grammatical speech. After all, a lot of people's salvation is at stake if Jesus Christ "ain't" Lord and Savior. Pastors and other academic theologians are ordained precisely to preach and teach accountably "the faith that was once for all entrusted to the saints" (Jude 3), regardless of whichever current ideological fad happens to be politically correct, however doctrinally deviant.

Lindbeck's concerns emerge directly from recent trends in both church and society. A generation of ecumenical dialogue has resulted in widespread claims of doctrinal reconciliation, yet without any accompanying capitulation or change. On the one hand, "propositional" religionists suspect dialogue participants of either self-deception or closet compromise. On the other hand, "experiential" expressions of religion (common in Liberalism) have also been replacing the more cognitive approach typical of traditional Orthodoxism. For most religious exponents of inner feelings and subjectivistic attitudes, ecumenical doctrinal convergences or agreements are considered irrelevant or misleading. Hence our present ecclesial stalemate.

As his alternative to both "propositional" Orthodoxism and "experiential" Liberalism, Lindbeck proposes a third approach that makes more understandable the intertwining of permanence and change, along with unity and disunity in matters of faith. He claims that doctrinal reconciliation without capitulation is a coherent and defensible notion only within a "cultural-linguistic view of religion" and a "regula-

---

[4]See my fuller review of George A. Lindbeck, *The Nature of Doctrine; Religion and Theology in a Postliberal Age* (Philadelphia: Westminster Press, 1984), in *LCA Partners,* December 1984, pp. 31-32.

tive or rule theory of doctrine." The aim of Lindbeck's book is to develop the conviction that the doctrinal dialogues of recent decades make better sense in this methodological context than in any other framework. Rules, unlike propositions or expressive symbols, retain an invariant meaning under changing conditions of compatibility and conflict.

For example, "Drive on the right" and "Drive on the left" are regulative principles or rules that are at once both opposed and yet binding—one in the United States, the other in Great Britain. They serve to control the differing spacial and temporal contexts of the theological "traffic" encountered. Unlike robot control, driving "safely within limits" (doctrinal orthodoxy) permits drivers a wide variety of flexible responses under different circumstances, while also demanding a healthy respect for clearly specified speed and space boundaries within the dynamic process being regulated.

So doctrinal rules and syntax of grammar are not merely (sociologically) normal, but (theologically) normative speech. They do not dictate any specific theological language; rather they set permissible limits and guide advisable options within those limits, in our own current choices of effective language.

Once again, to illustrate, Luther did not invent the doctrine of justification by faith because he had a "tower experience," of whatever kind. Rather, Luther's tower experience was made possible by his faithful response to God's self-revelation in the normative witness of the Bible. The Reformation was grounded not in Luther's subjective feelings about God, but in God's objective dealings with humankind (including Luther), as discovered through the evangelical exegesis of the biblical doctrine of the "bowels," or compassion, of God in Christ. In a "cultural-linguistic" model, religious experience and its multiform expressions are secondary, and even tertiary, to the primary objectivities of the religion in its language, doctrines, liturgies, and modes of action.

In a significant excursus on religion and truth, Lindbeck demonstrates his own orthodox integrity in acknowledging that, for Christians, "categorical adequacy" will not always meet the ultimate need for "propositional truth" when it comes to such basic affirmations of faith as "Jesus Christ is Lord." Distinguishing between the "truth of coherence" and the "ontological truth" of religious statements, Lindbeck freely admits that achieving the former is not a sufficient condition for attaining the latter. For epistemological realists, the "cultural-linguistic" model may well do the best job but still not the whole job. Some first-order truth claims of a religion do need finally to be cast in propositional form. Hence, the modest cognitivism or propositionalism represented by some classical Christian theists (e.g. Paul, Luther, Aquinas, rather than modern fundamentalistic literalists), while not implied, need not necessarily be excluded. Clearly, Lindbeck's characteristic fairness and irenic catholicity save him here from methodological fanaticism and even dogmatic heresy.

More recently, Lindbeck has also highlighted the hermeneutical helpfulness of the kind of evangelical catholic doctrine confessed in *The Book of Concord*. The Lutheran Confessions enhance our reading of the Scriptures and our hearing of God's living voice in them, by compelling us to concentrate on the central message of the Word of God. The Confessions, as John the Baptist, prove to be trustworthy guides precisely in their self-effacing Christ-centeredness: "He must increase, but I must decrease" (John 3:30). They authoritatively point beyond themselves to the

> source of that authority, on the metadogmatic trinitarian and christocentric doctrine of justification by faith. This is the criterion of all teaching and practice. Everything and only what the Bible mandates, permits, or excludes when read in accordance with this doctrine is mandated, permitted, or excluded. Changes take place in these scriptural instructions — God speaks afresh in new situations — but not in the interpretive rule. . . . One and the same doctrinal grammar generates an endless stream of novel sentences expressible in various conceptual and symbolic vocabularies.[5]

---

[5]George A. Lindbeck, "Confessional Subscription: What Does It Mean for Lutherans Today?" *Word and World* 11, no. 3 (Summer

It was in a similar spirit that Arthur Carl Piepkorn and Theodore G. Tappert lucidly interpreted the Lutheran Confessions for an earlier generation as norms for the proclamation of the church. In effect, they are answers to the question "What is Lutheranism?" As the *Epitome of the Formula of Concord* put it in 1577, the earlier Confessions—all written by either Luther or Melanchthon between 1529 and 1537—were officially endorsed by the Lutheran communion as hermeneutical testimonies that showed "how at various times the Holy Scriptures were understood by contemporaries in the church of God with reference to controverted articles, and how contrary teachings were rejected and condemned."[6]

Confessional subscription thus involves a public declaration of our commitment to preach and teach the apostolic Word of God under the guidance of those Confessions. In sum, taught Tappert, "when subscribing the Confessions today, Lutherans assert that, in view of the issues which were then at stake and the alternatives which were then offered, the Confessors were right. It is clear therefore that one cannot subscribe the Lutheran Confessions without affirming the Luther Reformation."[7]

It follows for Tappert that whoever thinks that the teachings of the Lutheran church are true simply because they are Lutheran *is* no Lutheran (K. F. A. Kahnis). Lutherans are not sectarian apostates. Their Confessional norms (*norma normata*) are themselves always to be governed by the church's scriptural norms (*norma normans*).

The Formula of Concord took pains to distinguish between the authority of the Scriptures and the authority of

---

1991): 317-20.

[6]Theodore G. Tappert, trans. and ed., *The Book of Concord* (Philadelphia: Fortress, 1959), p. 465, para. 8.

[7]Theodore G. Tappert, "The Significance of Confessional Subscription," *Essays on the Lutheran Confessions Basic to Lutheran Cooperation* (Lutheran Church-Missouri Synod, St. Louis, and The National Lutheran Council, New York, 1961), p. 29.

creeds and confessions. The latter are "not judges, like Holy Scriptures, but merely witnesses." The Word of God is and should remain the sole rule and norm of all doctrine, and "no human being's writings dare be put on a par with it." Alongside this clear distinction, it was also claimed that the teachings in the Confessions were grounded clearly in the Holy Scriptures.[8]

This normed-norm quality of the Lutheran Confessions under the apostolic Word of God commends their conscientious subscription and grateful use by the Lutheran church in today's pluralistic society. Especially at a time when the gospel's inspiration by the Holy Spirit is increasingly rendered null and void through the ideological opportunism and political correctness of a reigning "hermeneutic of suspicion," the Lutheran Confessions offer Christians an evangelical road map to get to the scriptural "cradle in which the Christ child is wrapped and laid" (Luther).

It is, after all, truly the gospel that is ultimately at stake. Moreover, it is not the gospel as merely one of the church's many different spiritual insights. It is rather the gospel as *the* vital heart pumping out evangelical blood to all of the other dependent organs embodied throughout the church catholic. Martin J. Heinecken always emphasized the Christ-centered unity of Lutheran Confessional identity.

> It must be acknowledged that the confessions are all of a piece and are to be understood as forming an organic whole from a central understanding of the gospel itself. In other words, they must be understood in the light of Luther's theology as constituting such an organic whole with its center in Christ. Luther was the best of "systematic" theologians because, although he never developed a complete system like Calvin in the *Institutes*, he was nevertheless marvellously consistent in his basic understanding of the gospel as he addressed it to the greatest variety of situations. So also *The Book of Concord*, although it does

---

[8]Ibid., p. 30.

not give a complete "system of theology," does present a consistent point of view over against certain opponents.[9]

Therefore the Lutheran Confessions can be an incomparable blessing for all current confessors of Christ, who are likewise determined to remain orthodox both in their message and in their mission. Authentic Confessional fidelity is not merely servile submission to the doctrinal laws of an authoritarian church (*sacrificium intellectus*); no, it expresses rather our grateful acknowledgment of the liberating gift of God's saving truth. Ultimately, it is a joyful privilege for an ordained minister to take solemn vows to remain faithful to the apostolic Word of God, as restored to its purity by the Lutheran Reformers.

Warren Quanbeck has summarized the chief benefits of such holistic Confessional subscription for a Christian communion that is committed to being both evangelical and evangelistic.

The Lutheran Confessions serve a threefold function in the church: (1) *doxology*—they articulate the church's confession of praise and thanksgiving to God for his saving work in Jesus Christ; (2) *hermeneutic*—they serve as standards and guides to the interpretation of the Bible in the church, showing how the Bible has been understood at certain critical times, especially with regard to theological issues in controversy; and (3) *identification*—they serve the self-identification of the church, indicating what things matter most in the life of God's people, and offering perspectives on the relationships of other concerns to those things that are seen as most important.[10]

In terms of current doxology, hermeneutics, and identifi-

---

[9]Martin J. Heinecken, "The Congregation of Word and Sacrament," in William S. Morris, ed., *The Unity We Seek* (New York: Oxford University Press, 1963), p. 129.
[10]Warren A. Quanbeck, "The Confessions and Their Influence upon Biblical Interpretation," in John Reumann, ed., *Studies in Lutheran Hermeneutics* (Philadelphia: Fortress, 1979), p. 177.

cation, it is my intention to employ one of the most important of the Confessions, Luther's Large Catechism, as the normative guide for critically evaluating the emerging convergence in ecumenical missiology today. Why the Large Catechism? Luther himself contended that the Catechism's five major parts—the Ten Commandments, the Creed, the Lord's Prayer, Baptism, and the Sacrament of the Altar—cover "the whole of Christian doctrine" and are deserving of our daily and lifelong devotional study. Indeed, Luther dared even to offer himself as a personal model to the many pastors and preachers who neglect the Catechism, "some because of their great and lofty learning, others because of sheer laziness and gluttony." He wrote:

> As for myself, let me say that I, too, am a doctor and a preacher—yes, and as learned and experienced as any of those who act so high and mighty. Yet I do as a child who is being taught the Catechism. Every morning, and whenever else I have time, I read and recite word for word the Lord's Prayer, the Ten Commandments, the Creed, the Psalms, etc. I must still read and study the Catechism daily, yet I cannot master it as I wish, but must remain a child and pupil of the Catechism, and I do it gladly.[11]

Luther also made it clear that the Catechism provides a Christian with "the rules and practices" of one's daily craft. The Christian faith is meant to be lived as well as learned, practiced as well as preached. To rout the devil, said Luther, we are to "eagerly read, recite, ponder and practice the Catechism" in meeting the demands and opportunities of informed discipleship.[12]

In light of this holistic standard in faith and life, it is imperative at the outset of our own textual analyses to acknowledge freely that the Large Catechism—as all the other Confessional writings in *The Book of Concord*—does not ever

---

[11]Luther's Prefaces, "The Large Catechism" in Tappert, trans. and ed., *The Book of Concord*, p. 358, para. 1; p. 359, paras. 7-8.
[12]Ibid., p. 362, para. 2; p. 360, para 11.

speak literally of the "mission" policies or the "evangelism" programs of the church, as we now commonly use these terms. Indeed, neither do the Holy Scriptures, our denominational extrapolations of the so-called Great Commission (Matt. 28:19-20) notwithstanding. The Lukan Pentecost account was totally unknown to the varied eschatologies in the books of Matthew, Mark, John, and Paul. That helps to explain why the subsequently divided churches have also so often been unable to agree in their conflicting and often competitive missiological visions and practices.

For Lutheran Christians who view their Scriptures and Confessions as norming and normed standards, this poses a doctrinal challenge that must be faced candidly, not least because of the checkered historical record of Lutheranism itself, precisely in the church's mission enterprise. Consequently, at least quickly in passing, we should note why this is generally so.[13]

First, Luther believed in the mid-1520s that he was himself living in the last days of "this age"—as did earlier his chief doctrinal mentor, the apostle Paul—and therefore he also anticipated the imminent return of the Lord in glory to consummate "the age to come." Consequently, Luther centered his own vocational efforts, in the expected brief interim before the end of the world, to restoring the purity of the gospel. Everything George W. Forell has so ably documented about Luther's expectation of the impending Day of Judgment as the "limiting principle" of his social ethics is equally applicable to Luther's truncated missiology.[14] Additionally, as we have already seen, the Lutheran Confessions were also then not composed as "constitutive" of a new church body to be designated as Protestant, but rather as "corrective" of the

---

[13]Historical sketches on the paradigmatic relations of Luther and early Lutheranism to missiology are developed prior to the current ecumenical paradigms analyzed below in the encyclopedic text of David J. Bosch, *Transforming Mission: Paradigm Shifts in Theology of Mission* (Maryknoll, N.Y.: Orbis, 1991), pp. 239-61.

[14]George W. Forell, *Faith Active in Love* (Minneapolis: Augsburg, 1954), pp. 156-85.

Western Christian church to be confessed as apostolic and catholic.

However, the Reformation failed in its proposed renewal of medieval Catholicism, and developed totally unexpectedly instead into the institutional expression of an independent "Lutheranism." As an unanticipated consequence, there then evolved a triple tragedy with respect to Lutheran missiology:

1. Sixteenth-century folk and state churches were doctrinally reformed, but then only quite inconsistently restructured for "emergency" survival, under the territorial and missional restraints of increasingly secularized governments, following the enforced abolition and then unreplaced missionary orders within the ex-Roman Catholic monasteries.

2. Seventeenth-century Lutheran Orthodoxy was actively opposed to any subsequent mission outreach, since its literalistic "propositionalism" restricted the "Go" mandate of the Great Commission to the original apostles, to whom, allegedly, it was exclusively and uniquely addressed.

3. Eighteenth-century Lutheran Pietism then both emulated and pragmatically cooperated with other Protestants in vigorous missionary activity by way of experiential protest against Orthodoxism, but generally under unofficial lay and/or agency extraecclesial auspices, and consequently often with eclectic doctrinal consequences.

Therefore, with only some notable exceptions—inspired largely by the nineteenth-century German Confessional renewal—the formative Lutheran missiological mind-set was disastrously shaped by successive periods of one-sided preoccupation with either (1) being evangelical but without becoming evangelistic, or (2) being evangelistic but without remaining evangelical. Their mutually divisive impact persists in the church down to this day, as demonstrated in current Lutheran debates on ethnicity, quotas, declining membership, the "church-growth" movement, revivalistic "crusades," religious "marketing," and even, oxymoronically, "entertainment evangelism."

There is obviously much of which to repent and even more from which to learn, in our Lutheran missiological heritage. My fervent plea is that twenty-first-century American

Lutherans respond confessionally to unprecedented challenges by viewing their "evangelical" and "evangelistic" commitments in complementary terms of "both-and" rather than an exclusivistic "either-or." We are the undeserving heirs of Luther's "theology of the cross," normatively and communally endorsed in *The Book of Concord*. Only Confessional fidelity can likely save us from our own belated drift into the doctrinal normlessness of American civil religion and/or pan-Protestantism.

Lutheran confessors today can and should use Christ-centered Confessions such as Luther's Large Catechism as plumblines of ortho-doxy (right believing) as well as life-lines for ortho-praxis (right living). We can work toward achieving a far more catholic synthesis of the inherent strengths in both Orthodoxism and Pietism by reverting to the deviations of neither (1) a pseudo-Confessional Fundamentalism that will permit the church to do virtually nothing as "mission," nor (2) a pseudo-Confessional Liberalism that will allow the church to do virtually anything as "evangelism." Those false alternatives are transcended in principle, once the Confessions are used properly to provide doctrinal norms for evaluating what is, and what is not, both permissible and advisable to adopt among the many current ecumenical theologies and strategies of mission.

To anticipate, illustratively, with the "vitalizing verbs" of Luther's dynamic development of the Third Article of the Creed, we too want to confess today that the Holy Spirit

(1) *calls* the church . . . to be an evangelistic community that is authoritatively entrusted and sent into the world with the good news of the Christ-event for all people;

(2) *gathers* the church . . . as an evangelical community that is centered in the adoration and praise of the triune God who is personally present in holy Word and blessed sacrament;

(3) *enlightens* the church . . . as an apostolic community that is scripturally and confessionally grounded in the same true traditional faith throughout the ages; and

(4) *sanctifies* the church . . . as a catholic community that is growing through divine gifts of regenerating grace, as a sign

and instrument of God's inbreaking reign and mission throughout the entire creation.

For the remainder of our study, therefore, we shall listen to the Confessions that they may guide us as a Confessing church. The two are inseparable. For while we are not bound to repristinate the historical record of any particular era, we are obligated to place all that the church is and does — including its part in God's mission — under those authoritative scriptural norms affirmed by the Lutheran Confessions. Therefore, in all that follows, a few characteristic features of current ecumenical missiology will be critically correlated with some central norms of the Christian faith, as developed in the five major parts of Luther's Large Catechism.

CHAPTER 2

Evangelical

"God Took Pity on Me"

THE SPRING OF 1513 WAS PROBABLY WHEN THE BREAKTHROUGH of God's Word concerning the righteousness of God finally took place in Luther's heart and mind. Significantly, both heart and mind were transformed, for both personal and doctrinal considerations were involved. Personally, Luther was still trying to find "a gracious God" by cajoling his Lord with virtuous deeds. "I firmly believed that I would have to continue to do good works until Christ was rendered gracious to me through them."[1] Doctrinally, he was troubled by the exegesis of certain verses in the Psalms that he had to treat in class lectures as Professor of Bible at the University of Wittenberg.

Luther feared and hated the term "righteousness of God" (*iustitia Dei*), which appears so often in the Psalms and the Pauline epistles, and it caused him great anguish. While diligently at work on Holy Scripture in his little room in the tower of the Black Cloister, Luther listened breathlessly as God finally spoke the living and forgiving Word to him. He later recalled:

---

[1]Martin Luther, *Werke; Kritische Gesammtausgabe*, 58 vols. (Weimar: Boehlau, 1883ff.), 47:590.

I was absorbed by a passionate desire to understand Paul in his Epistle to the Romans. Nothing stood in my way but that one expression, "The righteousness of God is revealed in the gospel" (Rom. 1:17). For I hated those words, "the righteousness of God," because I had been taught to understand them in the scholastic sense as the formal or active righteousness whereby God, who is righteous, punishes unrighteous sinners.

I raged in this way with a fierce and disturbed conscience, and yet I kept hammering away at those words of Paul, wishing passionately to know what he meant. After I had pondered the problem for days and nights, God took pity on me and I saw the inner connection between the two phrases, "The righteousness of God is revealed in the gospel," and "The righteous shall live by faith." Then I began to understand that this "righteousness of God" is the righteousness by which the righteous man lives through the free gift of God, that is to say, "by faith"; and that the righteousness "revealed in the Gospel" is the passive righteousness of God by which he takes pity on us and justifies us by our faith, as it is written, "The righteous shall live by faith." Thereupon I felt as if I had been born again and had entered Paradise through wide-open gates![2]

From this decisive moment on, Luther knew himself to be a person with a divine mission: ". . . to restore the holy Gospel once again." In wrestling with the very heart of biblical theology, Luther heard anew that eternal message of good news that had so fired the spirits of the apostolic church. He was recovering the gospel as "the power of God for salvation" (Rom. 1:16). Luther proclaimed the unconditional forgiveness of sin—and thereby new life and salvation—to all who have faith in Christ as the Son of God and the Savior of humanity. With this message, the evangelical catholic triumvirate of God's grace, Christ's cross, and human faith was restored to uncontested sovereignty within the church. How should that doctrine govern an evangelistic church in an ecumenical age?

---

[2]Ibid., 54:185.

Ecumenical Missiology: People of Other Living Faiths

DAVID J. BOSCH OF THE UNIVERSITY OF SOUTH AFRICA HAS published a monumental work entitled *Transforming Mission* (1991) that is likely to become a standard text in missiology for years to come. I shall hereafter gratefully quote, paraphrase, and summarize pertinent sections of Bosch's remarkable study, to provide the ecumenical context of my own critical analysis.

Part One outlines various New Testament models of mission, based largely on the eschatological views of authors of the Synoptic Gospels, Acts, and the Epistles, as well as the Book of Revelation.[3] Conflicting views on the time, place, agency, and manner of God's inbreaking reign—whether futuristic, realized, or inaugurated—have resulted in radically different missional stances among individual Christians and their corporate communities, both before and after the death and resurrection of Jesus Christ. The return of the risen Lord in glory did not occur as apocalyptically anticipated, and St. Luke was divinely inspired to write the Book of Acts precisely to help Christians to rethink and revise their missional mandate afresh in relating the kingdom of God to the church of Christ.

Part Two traces six historical epochs of mission that are presented in terms of so-called paradigms. These models describe how Christians dominantly perceived the church's mission in their own day, in view of both their changing understanding of the Christian faith and their changing responses to prevailing trends in their worldview and historical events around them.[4] These encompass the Eastern Church, the Medieval Roman Catholic Church, the Protestant Reformation, the Enlightenment, and the Ecumenical Era. While the final "postmodern" paradigm has not yet totally solidi-

---

[3]David J. Bosch, *Transforming Mission: Paradigm Shifts in Theology of Mission* (Maryknoll, N.Y.: Orbis, 1991), pp. 15-180.
[4]Ibid., pp. 181-348.

fied, Bosch in Part Three portrays a dozen intimately inter-related elements in an indivisible ecumenical missionary model, which he reports as now globally emerging.[5]

One such current ecumenical paradigm explored by David Bosch is viewing mission as *witness to people of other living faiths*.[6] The issue of nonbelievers is an ancient one, and we examine it first here because it has its roots already in the Old Testament.

Israel's covenant with the Lord God of Abraham, Isaac, and Jacob took place historically amid the prevailing cultures and religions of Canaanites, Assyrians, Babylonians, and other geographical neighbors in God's creation. For the purity of faith and life, being called out of the pagan world was considered imperative, only to be more intensified after the Babylonian captivity of the Jews in the sixth century B.C. " 'Therefore come out from them,' says the Lord," cites Paul, the apostle to the Gentiles, as the prevailing view of the Old Testament/Covenant that is also to govern the New: "Do not be mismatched with unbelievers. For what partner-ship is there between righteousness and lawlessness? . . . Or what does a believer share with an unbeliever?" (2 Cor. 6:14-15).

Throughout the Christian era up to the eighteenth-century Enlightenment, no salvation was acknowledged "outside the church" (Catholicism) or "outside the Word" (Protestantism). It was Liberalism that displaced this common model of "conquest and displacement" (sometimes military as well as spiritual), with a more relativistic attitude. As contacts and knowledge increased, serious Christians dis-covered in "other" religions an overwhelming array of both differences and similarities with Christianity.

What has become most striking for current "postmod-ern" Christians is the actual revival and revitalization of tra-ditional religions that were widely expected to wither away in the wake of Western science, technology, urbanization,

---

[5]Ibid., pp. 349-520.
[6]Ibid., pp. 474-88.

and secularism. However, it is increasingly noncredible today to juxtapose "the living Christ and dying heathenism." In various ways and to different degrees, both native religions and so-called great religions such as Islam, Hinduism, and Buddhism have demonstrated remarkable resilience. They have become more self-assertive and even expansionist. As one extreme example, Islamic fundamentalist terrorists and Arab nationalists have become linked inseparably in marching together throughout major parts of the world. In the final decade of the second millennium of its own expansion, the figures for Christianity are grim indeed.

> From the latest statistics available on the status of global mission, prepared for us by David B. Barrett, we learn that the percentage of Christians in the world's population has decreased slightly from approximately 34 percent in 1990 to 33 percent in 1991. . . . In Jesus' time the total population of the world was approximately 170 million. So we can say there were about one-sixth billion non-Christians at that time. Today, in a total world population of 5.3 billion, two-out-of-three persons, or 3.5 billion, are non-Christians. That is twenty times as many non-Christians as when Jesus preached the Sermon on the Mount.[7]

Bosch then documents how postmodern mission advocates, in confused response, remain theologically divided within at least three major schools of thought: exclusivism, fulfillment, and relativism. "Exclusivism" persists as the traditional missional attitude of conservative evangelicals (especially among those who opt not to cooperate ecumenically but gather together periodically as fundamentalistic "Evangelicalism" in such loose groups as the International Congress on World Evangelization).

Even in ecumenical circles, however, Reformed theolo-

---

[7]Gerald H. Anderson, "Foreword" in Gerald H. Anderson, James M. Phillips, and Robert T. Coote, eds., *Mission in the Nineteen Nineties* (Grand Rapids: Eerdmans, and New Haven: Oversees Ministries Study Center, 1991).

gian Karl Barth went beyond both Calvin and Luther in rejecting any general revelation of God in creation, and considered all nonbiblical religion as flagrant unbelief. Here, divine revelation was unalterably pitted against all human religion, with absolutely no "point of contact" between God and humankind remaining after the Fall.

"Fulfillment" is a second missional orientation that can lend itself well to such modern liberal approaches as adaptation, accommodation, and indigenization. Christianity then simply completes and perfects other underdeveloped cultural religious forms. However, this stance can also be assumed more ecclesially by the Thomistic (rather than Augustinian) branch of Roman Catholicism in testimony to the Scholastic dictum, "grace does not destroy nature, but fulfills it."

So, for example, the Jesuit Karl Rahner can even look upon people of other faiths as "anonymous Christians." Here it is affirmed that while salvation comes only through Jesus Christ, the cosmic impact of Christ as the Second Adam can and does permeate other faiths in varying degrees. Or alternatively, Joseph Sittler left Augustine for Irenaeus and espoused the cosmic Christology of the Greek Orthodox tradition. Sittler looked in hope for the recapitulation or uniting of humankind under the universal lordship of Jesus Christ, in witness to such biblical doxological passages as Ephesians 1:10 and Colossians 1:15-20.

"Relativism" persists as a third current missiological option, in direct lineage with precedents imbued with the spirit of the humanistic eighteenth-century Enlightenment. While extreme relativism is generally disavowed by postmodern Liberalism, Ernst Troeltsch's thesis still generally prevails. This posits an intimate bond between any given religion and its own culture, thereby effectively limiting Christianity's validity to a Western ethos. Bosch cites works of John Hick, Paul Knitter, and Raymond Panikar (who champions a Hindu-Christian synthesis) as strategically moving beyond Christocentrism to theocentrism in order to reject the finality and normativity of Jesus Christ and of Christianity for all peoples and cultures.

Bosch then argues for what he calls creative "theology of religions," which transcends the alternatives of "a comfortable claim to absoluteness and arbitrary pluralism." Endorsing the views of Max Stackhouse and Klaus Klostermeier, Bosch calls postmodern Christians (1) to accept the coexistence of different faiths and to do so not grudgingly but willingly, (2) to be genuinely committed to dialogue with people of other living faiths and ideologies, (3) to believe that in dialogue we expect to meet the God who has preceded us and has prepared the way for us, (4) to conduct dialogue and mission in an attitude of humility, (5) to recognize that religions are worlds in themselves that ask fundamentally different questions, and (6) to acknowledge that dialogue is neither a substitute nor a subterfuge for mission (as stressed by James A. Scherer).

Bosch finally concludes this important section with a candid statement of his own antisalvific convictions:

> Much of the debate about the relationship between the Christian faith and other faiths has been confounded by the perennial questions whether other religions also "save." . . . Such an ahistorical and otherworldly perception of salvation is spurious, particularly if one adds that all people have to do to attain it, is to subscribe to a set system of dogmas, rites and institutions.
>
> Conversion is, however, not the joining of a community in order to procure "eternal salvation"; it is, rather, a change in allegiance in which Christ is accepted as Lord and center [sic!] of one's life. A Christian is not simply somebody who stands a better chance of being "saved," but a person who accepts the responsibility to serve God in this life and promote God's reign in all its forms.[8]

In critical evaluation, we will turn first to offer some catechetical norms that were related to the Ten Commandments and the Creed by that prophetic reformer who identified as "the Gospel in miniature," the good news of Holy Scripture

---

[8]Bosch, *Transforming Mission*, p. 488.

that God sent Christ into the world as its Lord and Savior "so that everyone who believes in him may not perish but may have eternal life" (John 3:16). For Luther, the current discussion of "religious pluralism" would not be merely descriptive. It presupposes an ontological relativism ("*other* living faiths"), which is itself really a thinly veiled universalist negation of the church's salvific claims of God's special revelation through Israel and in Christ. Therefore authentic New Testament missiology must always be ready to confess boldly why it was deemed necessary by God the Father for the Son to be sent "in order that the world might be saved through him" (John 3:17).

Law Norms: The Ten Commandments

IN LUTHER'S LARGE CATECHISM, THE OPENING SECTION ON THE Ten Commandments does not deal explicitly with the church's missionary outreach to persons of (no faith or) other faiths. As we have seen, however, this is not surprising, because directly treating such missiological issues is not the intention of a manual of Christian doctrine. Catechisms concentrate on the basic rule of faith (*regula fidei*), which the church is then called by the Holy Spirit to contextualize and inculturate in the particulars of its own participation in God's mission.

Hence, Luther's purpose in the Large Catechism was to teach the teachers; that is, to provide a standard point of reference to edify poorly educated local clergy for subsequently developing their own congregational instruction in what Lutherans believe. Moreover, for maximal usage, Luther's contemporary explanations were intentionally less universal than the church classics but more general than local parish applications.

The Confessions can ably perform this normative service for our own missiology as well. To guide our current approach to nonbelievers, there are at least three evangelical insights to be learned from Luther's interpretation of the Ten

Commandments—climaxed in the Large Catechism—which he himself derived largely from the dialectical teaching of Paul. These are: (1) God's twofold rule of humanity by law and gospel, (2) God's twofold purpose in commanding a universal law prior to the Christ-event, and consequently (3) God's twofold revelation in creation and redemption— including persons of (no faith or) other living faiths.

1. God's Twofold Rule of Humanity by Law and Gospel

The Formula of Concord (1577) later believed it imperative to reaffirm:

> The distinction between law and Gospel is an especially brilliant light which serves the purpose that the Word of God may be rightly divided and the writings of the holy prophets and apostles may be explained and understood correctly. We must therefore observe this distinction with particular diligence lest we confuse the two doctrines and change the Gospel into law. This would darken the merit of Christ and rob disturbed consciences of the comfort which they would otherwise have in the holy Gospel when it is preached purely and without admixture, for by it Christians can support themselves in their greatest temptations against the terrors of the law.[9]

The Lutheran confessors also readily acknowledged that from a purely linguistic viewpoint, "the word 'gospel' is not used in a single sense in Holy Scripture." It has both a general and a narrow, both an inclusive and an exclusive, meaning. As we shall discover below, it is precisely this linguistic latitude that doctrinally veils so much unevangelical ideology in influential ecumenical approaches to mission and evangelism today. It is at just this critical point that the Lutheran *proprium* of God's law-free gospel has its place. The confessors made a

---

[9]Theodore G. Tappert, trans. and ed., *The Book of Concord* (Philadelphia: Fortress, 1959), p. 558, sec. 5, para. 1.

major doctrinal decision that was grounded in Luther's evangelical exegesis.

> Therefore we believe, teach, and confess that when the word "Gospel" means the entire doctrine of Christ which he proclaimed personally in his teaching ministry and which his apostles also set forth (examples of this meaning occur in Mark 1:15 and Acts 20:24), then it is correct to say or write that the Gospel is a proclamation both of repentance and of forgiveness of sin.
>
> But when the law and Gospel are opposed to each other, as when Moses is spoken of as a teacher of the law in contrast to Christ as a preacher of the Gospel, then we believe, teach, and confess that the Gospel is not a proclamation of contrition and reproof but is, strictly speaking, a comforting and joyful message which does not reprove or terrify but comforts consciences that are frightened by the law, directs them solely to the merit of Christ, and raises them up again by the delightful proclamation of God's grace and favor acquired through the merits of Christ.[10]

For Luther, the law and the gospel stand in dialectical opposition to each other.[11] In the soteriology of his "theology of the cross," law and gospel represent the two radically different ways in which the triune God relates to a fallen humankind. In explaining his Ninety-Five Theses (1517), Luther writes:

> According to the Apostle in Romans 1 (:3-6), the Gospel is a preaching of the incarnate Son of God, given to us without any merit on our part for salvation and peace. It is a word of salvation, a word of grace, a word of comfort, a word of joy, a voice of the bridegroom and the bride, a

---

[10]Ibid., p. 478, sec. 5, paras. 5-6.

[11]Earlier versions of material in this section may be found in my "Love and Law in Christian Life" in Carter Lindberg, ed., *Piety, Politics and Ethics: Reformation Studies in Honor of George Wolfgang Forell* (Kirksville, Mo.: The Sixteenth-Century Journal Publishers, 1984), pp. 103-17; and in my *Helping Youth and Adults Know Doctrine* (Philadelphia: Lutheran Church Press, 1963), pp. 39-45.

good word, a word of peace. . . . But the law is a word of destruction, a word of wrath, a word of sadness, a word of grief, a voice of the judge and the defendant, a word of restlessness, a word of curse. For according to the apostle, "The law is the power of sin" (Cf. I Corinthians 15:56), and "the law brings wrath" (Romans 4:15); it is a law of death (Romans 7:5, 13).[12]

Through the demands of the law, God accuses sinners of their unfaith and disobedience. Through the promises of the gospel, God grants faithful persons the forgiveness of sin, life, and salvation. Condemned by the law, sinners are crucified with Christ; redeemed by the gospel, saints are resurrected in Christ. It follows for Luther that Christian salvation and service can take place only when persons pass from the work-righteousness of the law to the faith-righteousness of the gospel. Hence the law serves the gospel, which is the primary form of the Word of God.

As early as his work *Brief Explanation of the Ten Commandments, The Creed and the Lord's Prayer* (1520), Luther was convinced of the evangelical interrelation of these three basic texts at the heart of his Catechism. He wrote:

> The ordinary Christian, who cannot read the Scriptures, is required to learn and know the *Ten Commandments, the Creed*, and the *Lord's Prayer*; and this has not come to pass without God's special ordering. For these contain fully and completely everything that a Christian needs to know, all put so briefly and so plainly that no one can make complaint or excuse, saying that what he needs for his salvation is too long or too hard to remember.
>
> Three things a man needs to know in order to be saved. First, he must know what he ought to do and what he ought not to do. Second, when he finds that by his own strength he can neither do the things he ought, nor leave undone the things he ought not to do, he must know where to seek and find and get the strength he needs.

---

[12]*Luther's Works, American Edition* (Philadelphia: Fortress, 1959), 31:231.

Third, he must know how to seek and find and get this strength. When a man is ill, he needs to know first what his illness is, — what he can do and what he cannot do. Then he needs to know where to find the remedy that will restore his health and help him to do and leave undone the things he ought. Third, he must ask for this remedy, and seek it, and get it or have it brought to him. In like manner, the *Commandments* teach a man to know his illness, so that he feels and sees what he can do and what he cannot do, what he can and what he cannot leave undone, and thus knows himself to be a sinner and a wicked man. After that the *Creed* shows him and teaches him where he may find the remedy, — the grace which helps him to become a good man and to keep the Commandments; it shows him God, and the mercy which He has revealed and offered in Christ. In the third place, the *Lord's Prayer* teaches him how to ask for this grace, get it, and take it to himself, to wit, by habitual, comforting prayer; then grace is given, and by the fulfillment of God's commandments he is saved.

These are the three chief things in all the Scriptures. Therefore we begin at the beginning, with the *Commandments*, which are the first thing, and learn to recognize our sin and wickedness, that is, our spiritual illness, which prevents us from doing the thing we ought to do and leaving undone the things we ought not to do.[13]

We hear echoes of St. Paul's apostolic overview of fallen humanity in Luther's prophetic interpretation of the Ten Commandments. It is likewise wholly consistent with the Augustinian view of original sin, which Luther so vigorously defended in his own earlier work, *The Bondage of the Will* (1525). It affirms at its core *lex semper accusat*, that God's "law always accuses" us sinners, whether unforgiven or forgiven, that we neither can nor will let God be God.

Luther applies to all Ten Commandments, though preeminently to the First, the awesome words that constitute its expository epilogue: "I the Lord your God am a jealous God,

---

[13]Martin Luther, *Works*, 6 vols. (Philadelphia: Muhlenberg, 1915-1943, 2:354.

punishing children for the iniquity of parents, to the third and the fourth generation of those who reject me, but showing steadfast love to the thousandth generation of those who love me and keep my commandments" (Exod. 20:5b-7). So there is a profound evangelical reason for Luther's designating the Decalogue as Part One of the Large Catechism:

> . . . The Ten Commandments do not by themselves make us Christians, for God's wrath and displeasure still remain on us because we cannot fulfill his demands. . . . Mankind is in such a situation that no one can keep the Ten Commandments perfectly, even though he has begun to believe.[14]

Following Paul, Luther develops the Decalogue, not in terms of the divine Creator's pre-Fall will of love (*Torah* or *Gebot*), but rather in terms of the divine Judge's post-Fall demands of wrath (*Nomos* or *Gesetz*), in the legalization of God's positive will into negative commandments. Luther clearly did not accept the Jewish tradition that designated Exodus 20:2 ("I am the Lord your God") as (part of) the First Commandment. Indeed, this gracious promise of God's covenantal love was added as a prologue to the Decalogue in some of the later editions of Luther's Small Catechism only after the Reformer's death.

In a fallen creation—seen fully only on this side of the cross—idolatry is our identity. So in the face of our infidelity, God is "jealous." The First Commandment says it all, and then goes on in nine other commandments to illustrate it universally before God and throughout society: "You shall have no other gods." Luther writes:

> A god is that to which we look for all good and in which we find refuge in every time of need. To have a god is nothing else than to trust and believe him with our whole heart. As I have often said, the trust and faith of the heart alone make both God and an idol. If your faith and trust are

---

[14]Tappert, *The Book of Concord*, p. 420, part 2, para. 68; p. 420, part 3, para. 2.

right, then your God is the true God. On the other hand, if your trust is false and wrong, then you have not the true God. For these two belong together, faith and God. That to which your heart clings and entrusts itself is, I say, really your God.[15]

This is exactly the meaning and right interpretation of the first and chief commandment, from which all the others proceed. This word, "You shall have no other gods," means simply, "You shall fear, love and trust me as your one true God." Wherever a man's heart has such an attitude toward God, he has fulfilled this commandment and all the others.[16]

2. God's Twofold Purpose in Commanding a Universal Law Prior to the Christ-Event

Why does Luther structure his Large Catechism in conscious opposition to the patterns of both medieval Catholicism (e.g., John Gerson) and later Calvinism (e.g., Heidelberg Confession), by treating God's law (in the Ten Commandments) not after but before the gospel (in the Creed)? Even more pointedly, why does Luther purposely use the Roman, rather than the Reformed enumeration of the Ten Commandments, and then carefully subdivide the two tables of the Mosaic Decalogue in such a way as (1) to combine the first three commandments on the first table in relation to God (*coram deo*), and then (2) to group the last seven commandments on the second table in relation to society (*coram hominibus*)?

Luther first developed his highly influential view of God's twofold rule by law and gospel in the realms of fallen creation and redemption in the work entitled *Temporal Authority: To What Extent It Should Be Obeyed* (1523).[17] In Luther's reading of biblical, especially Pauline, eschatology, the triune God rules all of life dialectically by the power of

---

[15]Ibid., p. 365, para. 2.
[16]Ibid., p. 409, para. 324.
[17]*Luther's Works, American Edition*, 45:75-130.

the sovereign Word. This takes place through the continual interaction of God's law and gospel, each with two complementary functions. As Redeemer and Sanctifier, God employs the gospel (1) to reckon the "righteousness of Christ" (*iustitia Christi*) to faithful persons in the realm of redemption, and (2) to empower the "Christian righteousness" (*iustitia christiana*) of loving persons in the realm of creation. As Creator and Preserver, God is at the same time employing the law (1) to prompt the "civil righteousness" (*iustitia civilis*) of rational persons in the realm of creation, and (2) to judge the willful misuse of "original righteousness" (*iustitia originalis*) by sinful persons in the realm of redemption.

Luther consistently taught that the law always accuses sinners, non-Christians and Christians alike, both in society (*coram hominibus*) and before God (*coram deo*). Of special interest to us is the incisive way in which Luther develops his view of the "double use of the law" (*duplex usus legis*) in his opening *Lectures on Galatians* (1531). He writes:

> Here one must know that there is a double use of the law. One is the civic use (*usus civilis*). God has ordained civic laws, indeed all laws, to restrain transgressions. Therefore every law was given to hinder sins. Does this mean that when the law restrains sin, it justifies? Not at all. While I refrain from killing or from committing adultery or from stealing, or when I abstain from other sins, I do not do this voluntarily or from the love of virtue but because I am afraid of the sword and of the executioner.[18]
>
> The other use of the law is the theological or spiritual one (*usus theologicus*), which serves to increase transgressions. This is the primary purpose of the law of Moses, that through it sin might grow and be multiplied, especially in the conscience. Paul discusses this magnificently in Romans 7.
>
> Therefore the *true function and the chief and proper use* of the law is to reveal to man his hate, and contempt of God, death, hell, judgment, and the well-deserved wrath of God. Yet this use of the law is completely unknown to the

---

[18]Ibid., 26:308.

hypocrites, the sophists in the universities, and to all men who go along in the presumption of the righteousness of the law or of their own righteousness.[19]

To protect Christian freedom from the continual threats of moralism and legalism, Luther then firmly concludes: "And that is as far as the law goes."[20] Therefore, in the Large Catechism, Luther treats the Ten Commandments before, rather than after, the Creed, because the twofold purpose of the law universally, i.e., as the human "point of contact" between unrighteous Christian and non-Christian alike, is to promote justice (ethically) and to expose sin (religiously).

The theological problem then arises: all this covers the Christian as a citizen in society and insofar as one remains sinful before God. But what is the role of the law for a Christian insofar as that baptized saint is already righteous before God? More concretely, are the "Thou shalt nots" of the Ten Commandments binding upon the Christian? Luther's startling response is typically dialectical: as Mosaic law—no; as natural law—yes!

This very profound view is developed most cogently in a decisive section of the work *Against the Heavenly Prophets* (1525). Luther has just concluded a defense of the freedom of evangelical Christians. They could either keep or destroy former Roman church images, depending on their state of faith and the state of local conditions. To answer Andrew Karlstadt's charge that such Christian freedom regarding church furnishings violates the letter of the Mosaic law, Luther replies vigorously that this does not concern him in the least! The reason: Christians who are under the dispensation of the New Testament gospel are not bound by the Old Testament dispensation of the Mosaic law. Christ has liberated us from the law—all of the law—from the minutest ceremonial nicety to the Decalogue itself. Says Luther, "For Moses is given to the Jewish people alone, and does not con-

---

[19]Ibid., p. 309. Italics mine.
[20]Ibid., p. 313.

cern us Gentiles and Christians. We have our Gospel and the New Testament."[21] Luther concludes that insofar as the Ten Commandments provide us with a concise statement of the natural law governing all of sinful humankind ("to honor parents, not to kill, not to commit adultery, to serve God, etc."), they are to be obeyed absolutely. But insofar as they include special matters above and beyond the natural law that are peculiar to the Jewish theocracy ("legislation about images and the sabbath, etc."), they may be regarded as time-bound statutes of the Jewish law code that are not binding upon Christians. Luther writes:

> It is when an emperor or a king makes special laws and ordinances in his territory, as the law code of Saxony (*Sachsenspiegel*) and yet common natural laws such as to honor parents, not to kill, not to commit adultery, to serve God, etc., prevail and remain in all lands. Therefore one is to let Moses be the *Sachsenspiegel* of the Jews and not to confuse us Gentiles with it, just as the *Sachsenspiegel* is not observed in France, though the natural law there is in agreement with it.[22]

The church instructs its members in the Ten Commandments, therefore, because "the natural laws were never so orderly and well written as by Moses."[23] In no instance should this practice be used to justify the reintroduction of any Judaic legalism in Christian daily living. Insofar as a Christian still remains sinful, one is bound only to that part of the Decalogue that coincides with the natural law (civil righteousness). Insofar as one is already righteous, however, that baptized saint is free from all law—Mosaic and natural alike—to live in the faith-activated love empowered by God's grace (Christian righteousness). Consequently, righteous Christians will find it continually necessary "to make new

---

[21]Ibid., 40:92.
[22]Ibid., p. 98.
[23]Ibid.

Decalogues as did Christ, St. Peter, and St. Paul," in responding faithfully to the Holy Spirit of the living God.[24]

Luther exercises this Christian liberty himself in his own doctrinal reinterpretation of the Third of the Ten Commandments, "You shall sanctify the holy day."[25] Sabbath observance on the last day of the week is deemed a distinctively Mosaic addition to the universal natural law that is embodied in the other nine commandments.

> Therefore, according to its literal, outward sense, this commandment does not concern us Christians. It is an entirely external matter, like the other ordinances of the Old Testament connected with particular customs, persons, times and places, from all of which we are now set free in Christ.[26]

Luther therefore reuniversalizes the meaning of the Third Commandment for non-Jews by shifting its natural law obedience from observing the Sabbath to ceasing from labor on a day of rest, thereby making a holiday of a holy day. This side of Easter, says Luther, we Christians can also celebrate Christ's resurrection on the first day of the week by dedicating some of this universal rest time to worship God together, and "to occupy ourselves with God's Word and deal especially with the *Ten Commandments*, the *Creed* and the *Lord's Prayer*."[27]

It is clear how deftly Luther fulfills a double concern in his evangelical interpretation of the law of God: (1) he makes no religious compromises with Judaic law on the law-free gospel (*coram deo*), while simultaneously (2) he makes common cause ethically with both Jews and all other human beings on whose hearts the essentials of God's natural law have been universally written (*coram hominibus*). We will show below how a far more nuanced implementation of this

---

[24]Martin Luther, *Werke*, vol. 39, 1, p. 47.
[25]Tappert, *The Book of Concord*, pp. 375-79.
[26]Ibid., p. 376, para. 82.
[27]Ibid., p. 377, paras. 88, 89.

doctrinal position could strongly shape our church's current evangelism and mission.

3. God's Twofold Revelation in Creation and Redemption

Building on the foundation of Luther's doctrinal insights into the Ten Commandments, what validity have the non-Christian religious and philosophical worldviews? How is God's personal revelation in Holy Scripture related to the general witness to God that is to be found in sin-corrupted creation, reason, and conscience? On the basis of God's twofold rule of humanity by law and gospel, as well as God's twofold purpose in commanding a universal law prior to the Christ-event, what should be the church's evangelism and mission to persons of (no faith or) other living faiths?

Paul provides Luther with the basic Christian approach to these problems as well in the opening chapters of his Letter to the Romans. Paul begins boldly with a proclamation of the gospel of God. The good news that God "promised beforehand through his prophets in the holy scriptures" has now been fulfilled in Jesus Christ. He is our Lord, "who was descended from David according to the flesh and was declared to be Son of God with power according to the spirit of holiness by resurrection from the dead" (Rom. 1:2-4). This gospel, furthermore, is declared to be "the power of God for salvation to everyone who has faith" (Rom. 1:16).

Paul then turns to analyze why the gospel of salvation is necessary for Jews and Gentiles alike. He insists that although God has left a divine witness in creation, persons have not responded in praise and gratitude. They have fashioned false gods with their self-serving reason. So instead of worshiping their Creator, they have resorted to sinful idolatry. All are guilty. Paul writes:

> Ever since the creation of the world his eternal power and divine nature, invisible though they are, have been understood and seen through the things he has made. So they are without excuse; for though they knew God, they did not honor him as God or give thanks to him, but they became

futile in their thinking, and their senseless minds were darkened. . . . they exchanged the truth about God for a lie and worshiped and served the creature rather than the Creator. (Rom. 1:20-22, 25)

Along with creation, rationally analyzed, Paul maintains that God has also left a witness to sinful humans in holy law. Although the Jews have known the will of God through the testimony of priests and prophets, they have continued to steal, commit adultery, rob temples, and vainly put their trust in their circumcision and physical descent from Abraham. Paul warns, "We know that the judgment of God rightly falls upon those who do such things" (Rom. 2:2, RSV).

Nor are Gentiles excused on this count because they have not had the benefit of Israel's written law. The Jewish law merely gives form to the universal moral law that can be discerned through conscience by all of God's creatures. The behavior of the Gentiles shows that "what the law requires is written on their hearts, to which their own conscience also bears witness" (Rom. 2:15). Paul is therefore forced to conclude that "all, both Jews and Greeks, are under the power of sin. . . . For there is no distinction, since all have sinned and fall short of the glory of God" (Rom. 3:9, 22b-23).

Paul's authoritative teaching provides Luther with his hermeneutical key for understanding God's self-disclosure in creation and redemption. Luther therefore summarized this position, during the same period as his own catechetical treatment of the Ten Commandments, in the parallel presentation of his *Commentary on Galatians* (1531):

> There is a twofold knowledge of God, the general and the particular. All men have the general knowledge, namely, that God is, that He has created heaven and earth, that He is just, that He punishes the wicked, etc. But what God thinks of us, what He wants to give and to do to deliver us from sin and death and to save us—which is the particular and true knowledge of God—this men do not know. . . . Therefore whoever wants to worship God or serve Him without the Word is serving not the true God but, as Paul says, "one who by nature is no god." . . . Apart from

Christ there is nothing but sheer idolatry, an idol and a false fiction about God whether it is called the law of Moses or the law of the pope or the Koran of the Turk.[28]

On the one hand, there is a general knowledge of God—apart from the Christ of Scripture. Through reason, creation, and conscience, all persons made in God's image can know something of God's existence, sovereignty, and righteousness. On the other hand, there is a particular knowledge of God—centered alone in the Christ of Scripture. He alone saves sinners. Through faith, all baptized believers can know of God's gracious and forgiving love. Christianity both judges (with the law) that which is truly idolatrous, and fulfills (with the gospel) that which is only partial in everyone's natural understanding of God. With persons of no faith or other living faiths, therefore, Luther would advocate a law-gospel twofold mission: (1) we cooperate ethically by struggling together for justice (in witness to God's universal law); as also (2) we continue to evangelize faithfully (in witness to God's particular gospel of salvation in Christ alone).

Ecumenical Missiology: Salvation and Evangelism

DAVID J. BOSCH DEVELOPS TWO OTHER POSTMODERN ECUMENI-cal paradigms in missiology with his presentations of the church's work in *mediating salvation* and in *conducting evangelism*. Exploring first salvation, Bosch recalls that the very name Jesus means "Savior" and that God's saving work in and through Jesus lies at the heart of the New Testament.[29] Yet the missionary enterprise of the church is necessarily governed by one's view of the scope of salvation: Is it personal or social; historical or cosmic; present or future; God-centered, Christ-centered, church-centered, world-centered, or person-centered? Once again, the shifting biblical paradigms

---

[28]*Luther's Works, American Edition*, 26:399-401.
[29]Bosch, *Transforming Mission*, pp. 395-400.

have inspired commensurate changes throughout church history in understanding the relation between church and mission, as well as the nature of salvation mediated by that mission. For the preceding modern era, response to the humanistic legacy of the eighteenth-century Enlightenment became both critical and divisive: Conservatives ignored it while Modernists embraced it. For the latter, "Luther's cry, 'Where do I find a merciful God?' is changed to 'How can we be merciful neighbors to each other?' "[30]

With the exception of the "Barthian interlude" of neo-orthodoxy (1920s to the 1950s), the modern period down to recent decades has witnessed numerous theologies of "secular salvation," which one-sidedly or even exclusively concentrate on human relations ("horizontal") at the expense of the divine-human relation ("vertical"). Advocates tend to treat sin as ignorance or alienation, salvation as the termination of unjust social structures, and then recast eschatology in terms of evolutionary optimism, development, and liberation.

These tendencies are traced by Bosch not only in the prevailing views of individual theologians and movements. They also came to dominate the official reports of such highly influential international ecumenical meetings as the Geneva Conference on Church and Society (1966), the Uppsala Assembly of the World Council of Churches (W.C.C.) (1968), and the Bangkok Conference of the W.C.C.'s Commission for World Mission and Evangelism (1973), with the latter's final report (Section II) characteristically developing the conference theme, "Salvation Today," exclusively in this-worldly terms: the human struggle for (1) economic justice against exploitation, (2) human dignity against oppression, (3) solidarity against alienation, and (4) hope and despair in personal life.

Comparing the competing claims of well-being and salvation, Bosch offers a perceptive summary of the church's postmodern missiological dilemma. He writes:

---

[30]Ibid., pp. 395-96.

To summarize, salvation and well-being, even if they are closely interlocked, do not coincide completely. The Christian faith is a critical factor, the reign of God is a critical category, and the Christian Gospel is not identical with the agenda of modern emancipation and liberation movements. We cannot, however, simply return to the classical interpretation of salvation, even if that position upholds and defends elements which remain indispensable for a Christian understanding of salvation. Its problem lies, first, in the fact that it dangerously narrows the meaning of salvation, as if it comprises only escape from the wrath of God and the redemption of the individual soul in the hereafter and, second, in that it tends to make an absolute distinction between creation and new creation, between well-being and salvation.[31]

On the basis of this postmodern challenge for the church's mediating a more comprehensive, integral, total, or universal "salvation" as the purpose for its mission, Bosch turns next to evangelism and to the resultant ecumenical chaos—both linguistic and theological—in recent attempts to come to grips with the New Testament realities of *euangelion* ("Gospel") and *euangelizesthai/euangelizein* ("preach the Gospel").[32] Bosch himself chooses to use the term *evangelism* to refer to (1) the activities involved in spreading the gospel or (2) theological reflection on these activities. He also employs the term *evangelization* to refer to (1) the process of spreading the gospel or (2) the context in which it has been spread.

In surveying the current world scene, Bosch states his own conviction that "mission and evangelism are not synonymous but, nevertheless, indissolubly linked together and inextricably interwoven in theology and praxis."[33] That, of course, poses the problem of "how" but does not attempt to solve it. In tones of neutral explanation, Bosch sketches, among both theologians and churches, four interrelated

---

[31]Ibid., p. 398.
[32]Ibid., pp. 411-20.
[33]Ibid., p. 411.

issues of controversy within two major areas of concern: (1) the differences (if any) between "evangelism" and "mission" and (2) the scope or range of "evangelism" itself. He sketches:

> First, some suggest that "mission" has to do with ministry to people (particularly those in the Third World) who are not yet Christians, and "evangelism" with ministering to those (particularly in the West) who are no longer Christians. . . .
>
> Second, there has often been a tendency to define "evangelism" more narrowly than "mission." And as Roman Catholics and ecumenical Protestants increasingly tend to use the word "mission" for an ever-widening range of ecclesial activities, . . . evangelicals began to avoid the term "mission" and to use only "evangelism," also for the "foreign" enterprise.
>
> Third, there has been, over the last four decades or so, a trend to understand "mission" and "evangelism" as synonymous. The church's task — whether in the West or the Third World — is one, and it is immaterial whether we call it "mission" or "evangelism."
>
> Further confusion was added when, fourth, the term "evangelism" or "evangelization" began to replace "mission" in recent years, not only in conservative evangelical circles but also among Roman Catholics and ecumenical Protestants. . . . [This is] either because of the colonialist overtones associated with "mission" [so the second and third groups], or because of the way that "mission" had been "re-conceptualized" by the W.C.C. at Uppsala 1968 and "implemented" as "new mission" at Bangkok 1973 [to the first group].[34]

In order for us to evaluate these conflicting ecumenical options extant today, we turn once again to the doctrinal norms confessed in Luther's Large Catechism, moving on from God's universal law of creation (Ten Commandments) to God's unique gospel of redemption (the Creed).[35] Postponing my own discussion of the Holy Spirit's sanctifying

---

[34]Ibid., pp. 409-11.
[35]Tappert, *The Book of Concord*, pp. 411-20.

work in the church catholic to the final chapter, I shall concentrate here on Article Two's affirmation of faith in "Jesus Christ, our Lord" because, says Luther, "the entire Gospel that we preach depends on the proper understanding of this article. Upon it our salvation and blessedness are based."[36] So great is Luther's concern for evangelical clarity in his Trinitarian orthodoxy, that he freely replaces the traditional Roman Catholic twelvefold subdivisions of the Creed with three simplified articles that highlight, by preeminent attribution, the indivisible work of the three persons of the triune Godhead: creation, redemption, and sanctification. For our own missiological focus on salvation and evangelism, the Second Article of Redemption deserves careful attention.

Gospel Norms: The Creed (A)

FOR LUTHER IT IS NO ACCIDENT THAT THE CREED'S SUMMARY OF the Christian faith does not include a single word on the teaching (to say nothing of the miracles) of the historical Jesus. After all, "the kingdom of God has come near; repent, and believe in the good news" (Mark 1:15) is the recorded common message of both John the Baptist and Jesus. What is finally unique about the Savior in the apostolic gospel is his person and work on the cross: "Jesus Christ and him crucified" (1 Cor. 2:2).

Calvary proves to be determinative for Luther as well. His doctrine has a soteriological center of gravity. As the Creed is the heart of the Large Catechism and as the Second Article on Christ is the heart of the Creed, so Christ's redemptive work on the cross is the heart of the Second Article. Luther's "theology of the cross" is governed by the apostolic gospel, which glories in the cross of the redeeming Lord. He writes:

> Let this be the summary of this article, that the little word "Lord" simply means the same as Redeemer. . . . That is to say, he became man, concerned and born without sin, of

---

[36]Ibid., p. 415, para. 33.

the Holy Spirit and the Virgin, that he might become Lord over sin; moreover, he suffered, died and was buried that he might make satisfaction for me and pay what I owed, not with silver and gold but with his own precious blood. All this in order to become my Lord.[37]

We see here the soteriological pulse of Luther's confession of apostolic doctrine. Christianity is not to be confused with an alternate form of the philosophy of religion; it claims rather to be God's way of salvation, pure and simple. The Pauline Gospel announces a saving event that has been graciously carried out by the Holy One who "proves his love for us in that while we still were sinners Christ died for us. Much more surely then, now that we have been justified by his blood, will we be saved through him from the wrath of God" (Rom. 5:8-9). (It is highly significant for Confessional "propositionalists" to be reminded here that Luther's teaching on redemption in this second article of the Creed does not even mention the Pauline doctrine of justification as such, but rather develops its evangelical equivalent throughout all three articles, thereby grounding soteriology eternally in the doctrine of the Holy Trinity.)

Luther reflects on this Pauline "good news" in doxological praise: "We could never come to recognize the Father's favor and grace were it not for the Lord Jesus Christ, who is a mirror of the Father's heart. Apart from him we see nothing but an angry and terrible Judge."[38] The gospel heralds Christ, and "Christ alone" (*solus Christus*), as the Son of God who was handed over to death for our sin and was raised from the dead for our justification or salvation. Luther then draws a stark conclusion from this doctrine of redemption that is directly relevant to our investigation of the church's current mission and evangelism. He writes:

These articles from the Creed, therefore, divide and distinguish us Christians from all other people on earth, whether

---

[37]Ibid., p. 414, para. 31.
[38]Ibid., p. 439, para. 65.

heathen, Turks, Jews, or false Christians and hypocrites, even though they believe in and worship only the one, true God, nevertheless do not know what his attitude is toward them. They cannot be confident of his love and blessing. Therefore they remain in eternal wrath and damnation, for they do not have the Lord Christ, and, they are not illuminated and blessed by the gifts of the Holy Spirit.[39]

I will postpone to the next chapter a fuller analysis of the evangelical catholic way in which Luther inseparably integrates the saving benefits of the body of Christ, both on the cross and in the church. Centered in the cross of Jesus and empowered by the gifts of the Spirit, the mission of the triune God is uniquely mediated through the apostolic mission ("sentness") of the one, holy, catholic, and apostolic church: "As the Father has sent me, so I send you" (John 20:21).

Our concluding task is simply and sharply to combine the doctrinal insights gained from Luther's interpretation of both the Ten Commandments and the Creed for strengthening our basic commitment to remain evangelical even as we become more evangelistic. Consequently, I submit that the Lutheran church will best act as the servant of God's twofold reign today through an *inclusive mission* and an *exclusive evangelism*. This means:

(1) an *inclusive* view of the church's holistic mission under God's whole Word (both law and gospel) in and for the whole world (both creation and redemption), as well as

(2) an *exclusive* view of the church's evangelistic mandate to proclaim rightly God's law-free gospel of "Jesus Christ and him crucified" for the salvation of sinners.

In contrast, for too much current ecumenical missiology, virtually everything that God does is indiscriminately subsumed under the "gospel," and practically everything the church does is uncritically included under "evangelism." It thereby substitutes a denominational church's personal law and social gospel for the Scriptures' universal law and per-

---

[39]Ibid., p. 419, para. 66.

sonal gospel. That serves only to "transubstantiate" the law and "memorialize" the gospel in the church's unique mission to save and to serve.

Christians are thereby tempted to expand "evangelism" beyond its authentic biblical limits at the expense of the "good news" of God's unconditional grace exclusively in Christ Jesus (*euangelion*). Nothing remains distinctively gospel when everything allegedly becomes "gospel." In opposition to our culture's neo-Gnostic and antinomian "cheap grace" (Bonhoeffer), we obviously need Confessional renewal.

On the one hand, we Christians are given the Great Commandment: "Love"! (Matt. 22:37-39). Love mandates that today's church endorse and carry out a vision of holistic mission ("sentness") that intentionally goes beyond evangelism in also witnessing to God's universal law. We should do so in critical cooperation with other persons of goodwill, regardless of their religious or irreligious persuasion, by joining in local and global struggles against evil forms of injustice, inequity, oppression, pollution, and dehumanization of any and all persons (and potential persons) created in the holy and loving image of God. The content of the church's mission ("sentness") is purposely not precisely defined in Scripture because it should always be in a continual state of creative redefinition, as every generation responds in faith-activated love and love-motivated justice to new challenges in a changing world.

On the other hand, we Christians are given the Great Commission: "Go"! (Matt. 28:18-20). Today's church should also be unswerving in its unalterable commitment to name the name of Jesus as the world's sole Savior. For Paul, the church's very reason for being is "to bring about the obedience of faith among all the Gentiles" (Rom. 1:5). God may well have other ways to us, but at least in the Scriptures and the Confessions, Jesus is our only way to God: "No one comes to the Father except through me" (John 14:6). In this christocentric fidelity, we joyfully proclaim to all who will listen, the personal gospel summarized in the doctrine of justification by grace through faith alone.

So while we certainly pray for church growth, we are not unevangelically motivated by "Church Growth," most especially if it is not an authentic expression of our obedience to "grow in the grace and knowledge of our Lord and Savior Jesus Christ" (2 Peter 3:18). In fidelity to Luther's "theology of the cross," we realistically acknowledge that an oak can grow slowly, while a cancer can also grow quickly! Whether due to our stubbornness or our endurance, Lutheran membership neither increases nor decreases as rapidly as most other denominations.

Ultimately at our best, therefore, we evangelical Lutherans are evangelistic because we can do no other. We are called into God's church and sent into God's world by the same Holy Spirit. We are saved both for the adoration of God and for the salvation and service of others, for Christ's sake alone.

> Therefore God also highly exalted him
> and gave him the name
> that is above every name,
> so that at the name of Jesus
> every knee should bend,
> in heaven and on earth and under the earth,
> and every tongue should confess
> that Jesus Christ is Lord,
> to the glory of God the Father. (Phil. 2:9-11)

CHAPTER 3

Catholic

"This Is My Faith, for So All True Christians Believe"

IT WAS BARELY A DECADE SINCE HE HAD POSTED THE NINETY-Five Theses, but by 1528 Luther fervently believed that both he and the world were soon coming to an end. Everything seemed at its worst for Luther: he was physically very ill and was sporadically tormented by what he considered to be demonic assaults (*Anfechtungen*); his voluntary pastoral duties multiplied as the Peasants' Rebellion was followed by a devastating plague in Wittenburg; his wife, Katherine, was suffering a difficult pregnancy, and their young son, Hans, was also sick; the elector was pressing for his personal leadership in a series of extensive visitations of evangelical parishes; his translation of the Old Testament prophets was badly delayed; and he was caught up in a nasty public controversy with some of his liberal Protestant opponents: Zwingli, Schwenkfeld, and Oecolampadius.[1]

Summoning all his ebbing strength, Luther composed a major refutation of the Sacramentarian heresies of his ene-

---

[1]Cf. Robert H. Fischer, "Introduction," Martin Luther, *Confession Concerning Christ's Supper* in *Luther's Works, American Edition* (Philadelphia: Fortress, 1959), 37:155.

mies in a work entitled *Confession Concerning Christ's Supper* (1528). Part Three of this "Great Confession" was composed as his theological last will and testament, as it were. Modeled on the Apostles' Creed, the doctrinal summary of the Reformer's beliefs turned out to be a major inspiration for the Schwabach Articles (1529) and in turn (together with the Torgau Articles), the magisterial Augsburg Confession (1530) itself. He wrote:

> This is my faith, for so all true Christians believe and so the Holy Scriptures teach us. . . . I pray that all godly hearts will hear me witness of this, and pray for me that I may persevere firmly in this faith to the end of my life. For if in the assault of temptation or the pangs of death, I should say something different—which God forbid—let it be disregarded; herewith I declare publicly that it would be incorrect, spoken under the devil's influence. In this may my Lord and Savior Jesus Christ assist me: blessed be he forever. Amen.[2]

Composed by Luther so soon before his Large Catechism, the Confession will deservedly receive more attention below. What must already be emphasized, by way of introduction, is the catholic substance of this work. Clearly intended as Luther's final credo (though God was to grant him another two decades of life), Luther's "Great Confession" placed him firmly and permanently in the apostolic tradition of catholic church dogma.

As Rome earlier found Luther to be too evangelical, so Zurich and Geneva now considered him to be too catholic—though neither opposing camp ever dared accuse him of tilting indecisively from some alleged middle-of-the-road position. As the early Luther refused to identify the church with Christ, so the later Luther refused to separate the church from Christ. In terms of classical Christian dogma, Luther consistently rejected the ecclesiologies of both the neo-

---

[2]Ibid., p. 372.

Monophysites in Italy and the neo-Nestorians in Switzerland by confessing the hidden lordship of Jesus: "I believe that Jesus Christ, true God, begotten of the Father from eternity, and also true man, born of the virgin Mary, is my Lord."[3]

It is essential to the evangelical catholic character of Lutheranism that the three ecumenical creeds of the ancient church were confessed on the very first pages of *The Book of Concord*. Luther remained an orthodox catholic in his lifelong fidelity to the Scriptures, creeds, liturgy, ministerial office, and baptized priesthood of the universal church's holy tradition. His sole aim was to fulfill the early church's Trinitarian Christology with a consistently evangelical soteriology. His renewal movement was essentially catholic, however antimedieval Roman. Luther always proclaimed that the finite can encompass the infinite when sanctified by the Holy Spirit (*finitum capax infiniti*). Therefore, it is Christ the Head who determines what is true of the church as the body of Christ. As God was bodily present in Christ (evangelical); so God's kingdom is likewise ecclesially present in Christ's holy catholic church, and God's Christ is also sacramentally present in the apostolic church's means of grace (catholic).

The "real presence"—incarnational, ecclesiological, and sacramental—says it all in the Spirit-blessed and efficacious "signs," "masks," and "veils" of Luther's christocentric Trinitarianism. His catholic piety affirmed:

> Nobody will obtain salvation . . . without external things. Attention must be paid to the Scripture, and Baptism must be sought. The Eucharist must be received, and absolution must be required. . . . The Holy Spirit works nothing without them.[4]

---

[3]Theodore G. Tappert, trans. and ed., *The Book of Concord* (Philadelphia: Fortress, 1959), p. 345, para. 4.

[4]*Luther's Works, American Edition*, 3:275.

Ecumenical Missiology: Church with Others and the Mission of God

IN GROWING TENSION WITH LUTHER'S EVANGELICAL CATHOLICITY, we turn finally to review the two most important elements in David Bosch's outline of the emerging ecumenical missionary paradigm; namely, the *Church with Others* and the *Mission of God (missio Dei)*.[5]

The changing role of the church in mission can best be illustrated against the background of Avery Dulles's ecclesial typology in viewing the church historically and theologically either as institution, as mystical body of Christ, as sacrament, as herald, or as servant.[6] Traditionally, claims Bosch, Roman Catholics and the Eastern Orthodox tended toward the opposite end of the ecclesial spectrum from Protestantism, which, "except for 'High Church' Anglicans and some Lutherans," tended toward a low view of the church, stressing the membership principle of voluntarism and the distinction between nominal church (*ecclesia*) and the true, little church as the bearer of mission (*ecclesiola*) within the large body.[7]

A fundamental paradigm shift has now occurred in the perception of the relationship between church and mission, says Bosch. On Protestant soil, this took place primarily through the contributions of twentieth-century world missionary conferences (e.g., Edinburgh 1910, Jerusalem 1928, Tambaran 1938, Willingen 1952, Achimota 1958, and Mexico City 1963). The breakthrough took place at Willingen, inspired largely by Reformed theologians Karl Barth and Karl Hartenstein.

> Willingen began to flesh out a new model. It recognized that the church could be neither the starting point nor the

---

[5]David J. Bosch, *Transforming Mission: Paradigm Shifts in Theology of Mission* (Maryknoll, N.Y.: Orbis, 1991), pp. 368-93.
[6]Ibid., p. 369.
[7]Ibid.

goal of mission. God's salvific work precedes both church and mission. We should not subordinate mission to the church nor the church to mission; both should, rather, be taken up into the mission of God (*missio Dei*), which now became the over-arching concept. The [singular] mission of God (*missio Dei*) institutes the [plural] missions of the church (*missiones ecclesiae*). The church changes from being the sender to being the one sent.[8]

Hence, by the time of the integration of the World Council of Churches and the International Missionary Council at the W.C.C.'s New Delhi Assembly (1961), "the church *is* the mission of God" had become the new ecumenical watchword of conciliar Protestantism.

During this same period, the Roman Catholic church was also, however hesitantly, coming to embrace a more missionary understanding of the church in such pre-Vatican Council II encyclicals as *Maximum Illud* (1919), *Rerum Ecclesiae* (1926), *Evangelii Praecones* (1951), and *Fidei Donum* (1957). The global (rather than Western) character of Vatican II helped the bishops immeasurably to move beyond the exclusively papal-centered ecclesiology of Vatican I.

This trend climaxed in the Council's *Dogmatic Constitution of the Church (Lumen Gentium/LG)*, whose opening words describe the church in terms of the mystery of God's presence in the world. With ecumenical sensitivity, the church is not simply identified with Christ, its Head. Rather analogously, "By her relationship with Christ, the Church is a kind of sacrament (*ubi sacramentum*) or sign of intimate union with God, and of the unity of all mankind. She is also an instrument for the achievement of such union and unity."[9]

That this reorientation was to be taken very seriously was underscored again by Rome in the subsequent Apostolic Exhortation *Evangelii Nuntiandi* (1975), which asserted, "While

---

[8]Ibid., p. 370.
[9]Ibid., pp. 371-72.

the church is proclaiming the kingdom of God and building it up, it is establishing itself in the midst of the world as the sign and instrument of this kingdom."[10]

In the emerging ecclesiology/missiology of both Protestantism and Catholicism, as envisaged by Bosch, the church is essentially missionary; it is not sender but sent. "Sentness" belongs to its very nature. Mission activity is not so much a work of the church as it is the church at work, participating in God's ongoing work. Carl Braaten is quoted in support of this basic reorientation: "a church without mission or a mission without the church are both contradictions, such things do exist, but only as pseudo-structures."[11] Guenther Gassmann reenforced this same viewpoint on the place and vocation of the church and its unity in God's plan of salvation. He quotes from the Report of the Faith and Order Commission at the W.C.C.'s Uppsala Assembly (1968): "The Church is bold in speaking of itself as the sign of the coming unity of mankind."[12]

However, at the same time, Ernst Käsemann challenged this sacramental view of the church as too triumphalistic. It is dangerous and almost frivolous, he said, not only because of the obvious lack of sacramental communion among the divided churches themselves, but also because they are then more likely to interpret the church as an "extension of the Incarnation" and thereby blur the abiding difference between Christ and the church. While a sacramental ecclesiology does still point beyond itself to Christ, Käsemann contends that the only legitimate sign of the church of Christ is the cross of Christ.

In this regard, it should also be noted how selectively Bosch quotes from Vatican Council II's *Lumen Gentium*. It is the same Dogmatic Constitution that is lauded for calling the church "a kind of sign and instrument of salvation," which then also, unmentioned, goes on to describe this same church

---

[10]Ibid., p. 374.
[11]Ibid., p. 372.
[12]Ibid., p. 374.

structurally in terms of the papal governance and apostolic succession subsisting uniquely with Roman Catholicism.

> This Church, constituted and organized in the world as a society, subsists in the Catholic Church, which is governed by the successor of Peter and by the bishops in union with that successor, although many elements of sanctification and truth can be found outside of her visible structure. These elements, however, as gifts properly belonging to the Church of Christ, possess an inner dynamism toward Catholic unity.[13]

Nevertheless, Bosch prefers to accentuate new perspectives of the relation between the church and the world that develop from the alleged Roman Catholic-conciliar Protestant "convergence" on viewing the church as sacramental sign and instrument in God's plan of salvation. Obviously the world is not viewed far more positively than merely as a resource of pagan converts for declining church membership. As Bonhoeffer viewed Jesus as the "man for others," so, it is claimed, we should view the followers of Jesus as the "church for others"; indeed, as a partnering "church with others." Thus, solidarity replaces subjection. Thereby it also stresses that the world is still God's creation; it remains the object of Christ's cross and the arena within which God still works outside the church.

Yet side by side with those ecumenical convergences on the church as God's mission, Bosch acknowledges that there also persists "an abiding tension" between two views of the church which appear to be "fundamentally irreconcilable." Why is this so? Partly it is due to the not-so-peacefully-coexisting older and postmodern images of mission, along with many mixed models, during a period of unprecedented world change and transition.

Even more deeply, however, as we have already discovered in our earlier discussion of the church's outreach to per-

---

[13]"The Dogmatic Constitution on the Church" in Walter M. Abbot, S. J., ed., *The Documents of Vatican II* (New York: Guild Press, 1966), sec. 8, p. 23.

sons of other living faiths, a good deal of our mission dilemma is grounded in the church's post-Enlightenment
biblical criticism. There we uncover a wide variety of conflicting biblical eschatologies that are now selectively defended by current partisans. Therefore, Bosch's final section
on the alleged emergence of a postmodern missionary paradigm ("Action in hope"), dutifully outlines a broad range of
eschatological options (dialectical, existential, actualized, sal-
vation-historical, and others), only to conclude in Lukan determination: "The disciples' being sent to the outermost ends
of the earth (Acts 1:8) is the only reply they get to their question about when God's reign would be inaugurated in its fullness."[14]

Can the church's "abiding tension" in missional outreach
at least be clearly described? In the hope of some kind of
eventual reconciliation, Bosch prefers not to pose the alternatives in terms of "either-or" but speaks rather of different
poles on a common ecclesial spectrum. He declares:

> At one end of the spectrum, the church perceives itself to
> be the sole bearer of a message of salvation on which it has
> a monopoly; at the other end, the church views itself, at
> most, as an illustration—in word and deed—of God's in-
> volvement with the world.
>
> Where one chooses the first model, the church is seen
> as a partial realization of God's reign on earth, and mission
> as that activity through which individual converts are
> transferred from eternal death to life. Where one opts for
> the alternative prescription, the church is, at best, only a
> pointer to the way God acts in respect of the world, and
> mission is viewed as a contribution toward the humaniza-
> tion of society—a process in which the church may perhaps
> be involved in the role of consciousness-raiser.[15]

The first pattern (identified largely with Protestant Fundamentalism) is today further exacerbated by the preoccupa-

---

[14]Bosch, *Transforming Mission*, p. 508.
[15]Ibid., p. 381.

tion with numerical church growth in some financially pressed Protestant circles. Bosch presents Donald McGavran's "church-growth movement" as illustrative of nonprophetic Christians who "rob the Gospel of its ethical thrust." Bosch says that their recommended "ethnically-homogeneous unit" principle, as institutionalized in local voluntary associations, only sabotages the church's universality.

> In this model, "achievement" in the area of mission or evangelism is frequently measured exclusively in terms of "religious" or otherworldly activities or of conduct at the micro-ethical level, such as abstinence from tobacco or profane speech. Often this also signifies a departure from engagement with the dominant social issues in a given community. Where this happens, an explosion in the numbers of converts may, in fact, be a veiled form of escapism and thus make a mockery of the true claims of the Christian faith.[16]

The second pattern (identified largely with elements of conciliar Protestantism and Liberation Catholicism) tends to "rob the Gospel of its soteriological depth." It manifests itself either (1) in an almost complete identification of the church with the world and its agenda; or (2) in extreme cases, a complete writing off of the church in the name of the world. Bosch depicts this approach reaching its recent Protestant zenith on the optimistic euphoria of the 1960s, most especially within liberal American Protestantism with its so-called gospel of *shalom* through societal humanization. The world was encouraged to "write the agenda" for the people of God. The leaders of this movement were the second-generation Barthian Reformed theologians who embraced, and then distorted, the "mission of God" (*missio Dei*) in order to subjugate the mission of the church not to God but to the world (cf. J. C. Hoekendijk, R. G. Armig, Ludwig Ruetti, and Colin Williams).

---

[16]Ibid., p. 382.

Bosch also sketches the prevalence of a similar "secular salvation" motif among some influential expressions of Liberation Theology (e.g., Leonardo Boff, Gustavo Gutierrez, the General Conferences of Latin American Bishops of the Roman Catholic Church). In reading the "signs of the times," Christians under stress are tempted to sacralize, selectively, particular sociological forces of history. Thereby they risk the earlier tragedy of the capitulating *Deutsche Christen* in Nazi Germany. In Latin America, horrendous societal conditions can lead a church virtually to identify God's inbreaking reign ("lo here and lo there") with the secular forces of Marxist ideology, economic development, revolutionary violence, community organization, and the salvific liberation of "the poor" or "the people" in a secular Utopia. Liberation, yes; salvation, no.

One leaves this major subject with the uneasy feeling that the "mission of God" (*missio Dei*) is at best a mixed blessing for current ecumenical ecclesiology—a danger that Bosch himself readily acknowledges. Nevertheless, he still unqualifiedly asserts, "It is inconceivable that we could again revert to a narrow, ecclesiocentric view of mission."[17] Is that necessarily so? One need not have a "narrow" view of ecclesiocentric mission, *if* the church is faithfully confessed to be the Spirit-empowered universal body of the Second Person of the Holy Trinity. At least for a Christocentric Trinitarian with a Pauline pneumatology, one can assert that God's kingdom transcends the institutional boundaries of Christ's church yet still boldly confess that it is nevertheless centered within it.

The crying need for Lutheran Confessional norms now emerges in bold relief, if our church is to remain truly evangelical while becoming more evangelistic. In the final pages of his almost six hundred-page encyclopedic survey, David Bosch charges that "the Western church has been tempted to read the Gospels—in Kaehler's famous phrase—as 'passion stories with extensive introductions' . . . [This phrase] be-

---

[17]Ibid., p. 393.

trays the preoccupation of the Western church—Catholic and Protestant—with the passion and crucifixion of Jesus."[18]

Well, liberal conciliar Protestantism is certainly not going to succumb to this "temptation" if that is what it truly is! For in covering Bosch's 175-page summary of essential elements of the "postmodern mission paradigm," one searches the index in vain for a solitary reference to either sin or the sacraments. Not one! If this vision prevails, the ecumenical missional future will likely be neither evangelical nor catholic.

It is within this soteriological wasteland that the churchly character of the mission of God in Lutheranism must either stand or fall. Sin and grace constitute the heart of the church's evangelization. It is on behalf of the Lord of the church that baptized and ordained priests of the church proclaim the church's gospel of God's atoning grace in Christ's cross. No gospel, no church; no church, no gospel. It is therefore high time for us to substantiate these claims, however briefly, by developing the norms of Luther's ecclesiology, sacramentology, and eschatology in the remaining parts of his Large Catechism.

Church Norms: The Creed (B), The Lord's Prayer, Baptism, Sacrament of the Altar

SANCTIFICATION, OR MAKING HOLY THE UNHOLY, IS THE WORK OF the triune God preeminently attributed to the Holy Spirit in Luther's interpretation of the Third Article of the Creed. Luther's doctrine of the church is governed by the sanctifying activity of the Holy Spirit through divinely ordained means of grace. As in Christ, so in the church of Christ: the finite encompasses the infinite in the power of the Spirit.

Luther treats "the holy Christian church" and "the communion of saints" as synonymous. The Holy Spirit makes "saints" (holy ones) by testifying about Jesus Christ: "he first

---

[18]Ibid., p. 513.

leads us into his holy community, placing us in the bosom of the church, where he preaches to us and brings us to Christ."[19] What God has graciously done *for us* in Jesus Christ must now be faithfully received *in us* through the Holy Spirit. "In order that this treasure might not be buried but put to use and enjoyed, God has caused the Word to be published and proclaimed, in which he has given the Holy Spirit to offer and apply to us this treasure of salvation."[20]

So for Luther, the scriptural ordering of the affirmations of faith in the Third Article is providentially ecclesiocentric: first the life-giving Holy Spirit proclaims the gospel; then is born the holy Christian church or the "communion of saints," who have been vivified by the gospel and granted God's gracious gifts of forgiveness, resurrection, and eternal life.

Luther summarizes his evangelical catholic understanding of salvation by the Holy Spirit within the Christian church under four headings. *First, the church is unique by virtue of its Head, Jesus Christ.* It is the incomparable workplace of the Holy Spirit who, with the Word of God, grants forgiven sinners the gift of faith to enable them to confess the saving lordship of Jesus Christ. It is the Holy Spirit who speaks "in, with, and under" the preacher's faithful proclamation of the living Word of God (*viva vox evangelii*). An evangelical sermon becomes a redeeming and sanctifying means of grace precisely because "faith comes from what is heard, and what is heard comes by the preaching of Christ" (Rom. 10:17, RSV). So, for Luther, no Spirit, no Word; no Word, no church; no church, no salvation. The Holy Spirit

> . . . has a unique community in the world. It is the mother that begets and bears every Christian through the Word of God. The Holy Spirit reveals and preaches that Word, and by it illumines and kindles hearts so that they grasp and accept it, cling to it, and persevere in it. . . . For where Christ is not preached, there is no Holy Spirit to create,

---

[19]Tappert, *The Book of Concord*, p. 415, para. 37.
[20]Ibid., p. 415, para. 38.

call, and gather the Christian church, and outside it no one can come to the Lord Jesus Christ.[21]

Second, the holy Christian church is to be understood as a communion, or community, of saints. It is a holy Christian people gathered about God's Word in order to become strong in the faith and in the fruit of the Spirit. "Until the last day," it is an anticipatory and efficacious sign of God's sanctifying reign in Christ through the power of the Spirit. This is the "sum and substance" of the "communion of saints" for Luther.

I believe that there is on earth a little holy flock or community of pure saints under one head, Christ. It is called together by the Holy Spirit in one faith, mind, and understanding. It possesses a variety of gifts, yet is united in love without sect or schism . . . until the last day the Holy Spirit remains with the holy community or Christian people. Through it he gathers us, using it to teach and preach the Word. By it he creates and increases sanctification, causing it daily to grow and become strong in the faith and in the fruits of the Spirit.[22]

Luther views the church here in eschatological conflict with God's created but fallen world. On the one hand, the church is certainly "a little holy flock" under its Head, Jesus Christ. It will not idolatrously pander to survive. On the other hand, God has raised Jesus from the dead and will continue to act as the Holy Spirit, "causing it daily to grow." So there are also divine grounds for churchly hope as God's people remain faithful. In a "theology of the cross," however, we dare not confuse eschatological hope and ecclesiastical optimism. God's true church—as God's true Son—is always hidden to all but the eyes of faith. In a "theology of the cross," divine victories usually look like human defeats, just as human defeats miraculously turn into divine victories amid a sinful and fallen world.

---

[21]Ibid., p. 416, paras. 42, 45.
[22]Ibid., p. 417, paras. 51, 53.

Third, the Spirit's work of increasing human holiness in the Christian church concentrates on the forgiveness of sin. Christ's victory on the cross has dethroned but not destroyed human sin. Outside the church, it still reigns; inside the church, sin no longer reigns, but its all-pervasive persistence in the life of the redeemed is in need of daily forgiveness.

In terms of our search for mission norms, Luther helpfully clarifies that "outside the Christian church" here really means "where the gospel is not." God's inbreaking reign is sacramentally centered in, but not structurally limited to, the divided and broken institutionalized churches that all call themselves "Christian." So Luther is not speaking ecclesiastically about institutional church membership as such. Rather he is witnessing ecclesiologically to the impact of the gospel in the kingdom of Christ, whatever its hidden boundaries in the world. Hence Luther could also consistently affirm a non-Roman but nevertheless catholic view of the ecclesial dictum of St. Cyprian: "outside the church no salvation" (*extra ecclesiam nulla salus*).[23]

> Further we believe that in this Christian church we have the forgiveness of sins, which is granted through the holy sacraments and absolution as well as through all the comforting words of the entire Gospel. . . . Meanwhile, since holiness has begun and is growing daily, we await the time when our flesh will be put to death, will be buried with all its uncleanness, and will come forth gloriously and arise complete in perfect holiness in a new, eternal life. Now we are only halfway pure and holy. The Holy Spirit must continue to work in us through the Word. . . .[24]

Finally, it is important for our missional outreach to hear Luther's doctrinal witness to "the resurrection of the body and life everlasting." Christ's work of redemption is already an accomplished reality, but the Spirit's work of sanctification is

---

[23]Ibid., p. 418, para. 56.
[24]Ibid., p. 417, paras. 54, 57, 58.

not yet completed. Through the Word and by the Spirit, more persons are to be brought into the community of saints. Clearly it is the unique pneumatological mission of God (*missio Dei*) to speak and work through the church, to build it up, and to guide its mission throughout history into eternity. Luther writes:

> Creation is past and redemption is accomplished, but the Holy Spirit carries on his work unceasingly until the last day. For this purpose he has appointed a community on earth, through which he speaks and does all his work. For he has not yet gathered together all his Christian people, nor has he completed the granting of forgiveness. . . . We now await in faith for this to be accomplished through the Word.[25]

We turn next to Luther's treatment of the Lord's Prayer in his Large Catechism for any doctrinal norms that will assist us in our evangelical reaffirmation of evangelistic mission outreach. Traditionally, attention has focused on the Prayer's second petition ("Thy kingdom come"). Lutheran missional piety has been immeasurably shaped by the memorization of its meaning in Luther's concurrent Small Catechism by many generations of children in catechetical classes throughout the world: "To be sure, the kingdom of God comes of itself, without our prayer, but we pray in this petition that it may also come to us."[26]

Luther's sole intention here was to reassert God's eternal sovereignty over against all human, even Christian, synergistic salvation. It was not written, as often wrongly interpreted, as an endorsement of missional apathy. Nor, under this second petition, was Luther forbidding the church to engage in social ministry or food distributions to the poor when he lauded the magnitude of God's eternal reign: "You see that we are praying here not for a crust of bread or for a

---

[25]Ibid., p. 419, paras. 61, 62.
[26]Ibid., p. 346.

temporal, perishable blessing, but for an eternal, priceless treasure and everything that God himself possesses."[27]

The provision of God-pleasing social justice and economic well-being, however, is normally the province of civil authorities and responsible citizens under God's universal law, as Luther goes on to insist under the Prayer's fourth petition ("Give us this day our daily bread"):

> To put it briefly, this petition includes everything that belongs to our entire life in this world; only for its sake do we need daily bread . . . food and clothing . . . peace and concord . . . in short, everything that pertains to the regulation of our domestic and our political affairs. . . .
>
> It would therefore be fitting if the coat-of-arms of every upright prince were emblazoned with a loaf of bread instead of a lion or a wreath of rue, or if a loaf of bread were stamped on coins, to remind both princes and subjects that through the office of the princes we enjoy protection and peace and that without them we would not have the steady blessing of daily bread.[28]

These twin caveats aside, however, it does remain demonstrably true that Luther devotes less than two pages to the subject of the "kingdom of God" in this second petition. Nor is there a single mention of "God's kingdom" in any of the rest of Luther's writings in *The Book of Concord*, illustrative of his eschatological stance in general. In Luther's Christocentric Trinitarianism, the kingdom of God is messianically personified by the crucified and risen Lord, Jesus Christ (*autobasileia*), and inaugurated in the body of Christ, the church. This is likely a direct reflection of the Reformer's dependence on Pauline, rather than Synoptic ecclesiology and eschatology. In any case, there is absolutely no theological evidence to substantiate any current claim that Luther "anticipates the present-day line of missiological thinking

---

[27]Ibid., p. 427, para. 55.
[28]Ibid., p. 430, paras. 73, 75.

which takes the kingdom of God, rather than the church [*sic*], as its key concept."[29]

In a word, when Luther is asked about the meaning of "God's kingdom" for Christians in the Lord's Prayer, he refers us directly back to our already-reviewed articles on redemption and sanctification in the Creed.

> What is the kingdom of God? Answer: Simply what we learned in the Creed, namely, that God sent his Son, Christ our Lord, into the world to redeem and deliver us from the power of the devil and to bring us to himself and rule us as a king of righteousness, life, and salvation against sin, death, and an evil conscience. To this end he also gave his Holy Spirit to teach us this through his holy Word and to enlighten and strengthen us in faith by his power.
>
> God's kingdom comes to us in two ways: first, it comes here, in time, through the Word and faith, and secondly, in eternity, it comes through the final revelation.[30]

In moving on now from Luther's identical treatment of ecclesiology and eschatology in the Creed and the Lord's Prayer, we need to pause a moment to highlight another distinctive and highly underrated feature of the structure of Luther's Large Catechism. While the medieval church had used written catechisms of various sorts for centuries before the Reformation, the standard parts covered the Creed, the Ten Commandments, and the Our Father (*Pater Noster*). This was also true of Luther's popular instruction in his own catechetical sermons and essays, beginning as far back as 1516.[31]

However, from 1525 on, Luther creatively expanded the traditional tripartite pattern of a catechism to include also "the two sacraments instituted by Christ . . . because without

---

[29]James A. Scherer, *Gospel, Church and Kingdom: Comparative Studies in World Mission Theology* (Minneapolis: Augsburg, 1987), p. 55.
[30]Tappert, *The Book of Concord*, p. 426, para. 51.
[31]Ibid., p. 357.

these no one can become a Christian."[32] By affording the church's sacraments such doctrinal prominence, Luther was making a major statement about their eschatological significance from an evangelical catholic perspective.

We recall that Luther had earlier relocated the Ten Commandments before the Creed at the opening of the Catechism in order to protect the church's law-free gospel. Following the cataclysmic events of the 1520s (which were wrongly interpreted apocalyptically), Luther's Large Catechism first introduced the church's two sacraments with awesome eschatological overtones. Moreover, Luther significantly placed them after the pre-Easter Lord's Prayer, precisely in order to amplify his own Pauline post-Easter eschatology. This side of the Lord's return in glory, the churchly inauguration of "God's kingdom" was now confessionally developed in terms of "Christ's kingdom," in Luther's (and Melanchthon's) portrayal of our baptismal lifestyle: "The church is the kingdom of Christ, the opposite of the kingdom of the devil."[33]

The fulfillment of "Thy kingdom come" is divinely inaugurated within human history by the crucified and risen Christ through the power of the Spirit. Thereafter, the church's law-free gospel is likewise made visible to the eyes of faith in the church's "new covenant" sacraments of Baptism and the Sacrament of the Altar. Here we have arrived at the catechetical climax of the mature Luther's eschatologically energized eucharistic ecclesiology. This was already prefigured in his personal "Great Confession" of the previous year (1528). He wrote:

> In this Christian Church, wherever it exists, is to be found the forgiveness of sins, i.e., a kingdom of grace and of true pardon. For in it are found the gospel, baptism, and the sacrament of the altar, in which the forgiveness of sins is offered, obtained, and received. Moreover, Christ and his

---

[32]Ibid., p. 436, para. 1.
[33]Cf. Wilhelm Maurer, *Historical Commentary on the Augsburg Confession*, pp. 262-66; Tappert, *The Book of Concord*, p. 170, para. 16.

Spirit and God are there. Outside this Christian Church there is no salvation or forgiveness of sins, but everlasting death and damnation. Even though there may be a magnificent appearance of holiness and many good works, it is all in vain.[34]

For Luther, the sacraments visibly proclaim the gospel. They are the Spirit's efficacious signs of God's unconditional favor toward us. They eschatologically link heaven and earth through the real presence of the risen Christ. They are the holy things that make the holy ones into the "communion of saints." Our sacramental communion with God in Christ through the Spirit always precedes and empowers our ethical communion with each other.

So a sacramental church is not merely a human religious organization, a voluntary association with optional rites and ceremonies. Inhabited by its living Lord, the church is a divine organism that takes on human organizational form in history—precisely through the sacraments. While not the whole catholic church, each local eucharistic community is still wholly the catholic church. Along with the Word and never apart from the Word, it is the sacramental body of Christ that organically constitutes the ecclesial body of Christ. There God the Spirit makes saints out of sinners through sermons and sacraments. So in response to the attacks of the liberal Protestant Sacramentarians, the mature Luther found himself driven ever more deeply into a Pauline-inspired eucharistic ecclesiology: the church is the body of the body of Christ (1 Cor. 10–11).

It now remains for us to document this controlling ecclesiological confession of Christ's "real presence" (*realis presentia Christi*) in Luther's concluding catechetical texts. Both the fourth part on Baptism and the fifth part on the Sacrament of the Altar are organized for simplicity by Luther around three central questions: (1) What is it? (2) What are its benefits? and (3) Who is to receive it?

---

[34]*Luther's Works; American Edition*, 37:368.

1. *What is it?* In terms of our evangelistic focus, what is most illuminating is that for the biblical foundations of Baptism, Luther couples together (1) the missiological command of Matthew 28:19 ("Go therefore and make disciples of all nations, baptizing them in the name of the Father and of the Son and of the Holy Spirit") with (2) the eschatological promise of Mark 16:16 ("He who believes and is baptized will be saved; but he who does not believe will be condemned," RSV).[35]

It is this "command and promise" dialectic of God's Word that is foundational for Luther. The church's Baptism is nothing less than "of divine origin . . . instituted by God himself . . . which God institutes and commands."[36] It is "not simply common water, but water comprehended in God's Word and commandment and santified by them."[37] Transcending a mere rite of the institutional church, Baptism is "truly God's own act."[38] It is a sacrament, a visible form of God's Word, "which contains and conveys all the fullness of God."[39]

> From the Word it derives its nature as a sacrament, as St. Augustine taught, "*Accedat verbum ad elementum et fit sacramentum.*" This means that when the Word is added to the element or the divine substance, it becomes a sacrament, that is a holy, divine thing and sign.[40]

As for the Sacrament of the Altar, its biblical foundation is Luther's conflated account of Christ's words of institution from Paul and the Synoptic Gospels (1 Cor. 11:23-25; Matt. 26:26-28; Mark 14:22-24; Luke 22:19-20).[41] We now under-

---

[35]Tappert, *The Book of Concord*, p. 437, paras. 3-4.
[36]Ibid., p. 437, paras. 6, 7.
[37]Ibid., p. 438, para. 14.
[38]Ibid., p. 437, para. 10.
[39]Ibid., p. 438, para. 17.
[40]Ibid., p. 438, para. 18.
[41]Ibid., p. 447, para. 3.

stand more fully the ecclesially catholic significance of the way in which Luther characteristically unifies (1) Pauline eschatology ("new testament/covenant in my blood" (1 Cor. 11:25) with (2) Matthean soteriology ("for the forgiveness of sins" (Matt. 26:28), without citing (3) the accompanying apocalyptic passage, "until that day when I drink it new in the kingdom of God" (Mark 14:25; Luke 22:18).

As in the case of Baptism, God's Word in ordinance or command in the Lord's Supper "is the chief thing to be considered," because it was "instituted by Christ."[42]

> It is the true body and blood of the Lord Jesus Christ in and under the bread and wine which we Christians are commanded by Christ's word to eat and drink. . . . It is bread and wine comprehended in God's Word and connected with it.[43]

---

[42]Ibid., p. 442, paras. 4, 5. Luther's historically conditioned concentration here on the "chief thing" does not mean that it is the "only thing" to be considered. Our Confessional respect for this normative soteriological criterion in no way precludes the current Lutheran church's further catholic recovery of compatible, recent, ecumenical, doctrinal, and pastoral convergences on the Lord's Supper, as summarized in the official worldwide Lutheran church responses to *Baptism, Eucharist and Ministry, 1982-1990; Report on the Process and Responses*, Faith and Order Paper No. 149 (Geneva: World Council of Churches, 1992). These include "the regaining of the Eucharist (Word and Sacrament) as the central place for personal and communal faith and witness, the development of a broader, comprehensive Trinitarian understanding in terms of praise and thanksgiving (sacrifice), the cosmic dimension, the ethical implications, the elements of reconciliation and participatory fellowship (*koinonia*), the significance of the memorial of Christ (*anamnesis*) and the invocation of the Holy Spirit (*epiklesis*), and the concern for more frequent celebration and receiving of the Eucharist, respect for the elements, distribution to the sick and admission of baptized children to the table of the Lord" (pp. 98-99).
[43]Ibid., p. 422, paras. 8, 9.

The words "in and under" convey Luther's sacramental realism in catholic depth. His position was also boldly reaffirmed in the Augsburg Confession ("really present . . . under the form of bread and wine").[44] The "real presence" of the bodily risen and exalted Christ is localized for us "in and under" the sacramental elements. The human incarnation of the Son of God is eternally indissoluble, for his human and divine natures are indivisible. Hence, the sacramental body of Christ is at the very heart of the ecclesial body of Christ. Thereby Luther had a firm biblical foundation to oppose both (current) Donatists and (future) Calvinists: "Even though a knave should receive or administer it, it is the true sacrament (that is, Christ's body and blood) just as truly as when one uses it worthily. For it is not founded on the holiness of men but on the Word of God" (cf. *manducatio oralis et impiorum*).[45]

2. *What are its benefits?* Luther teaches, "To put it most simply, the power, effect, benefit, fruit and purpose of Baptism is to save. . . . To be saved, we know, is nothing else than to be delivered from sin, death and the devil and to enter into the kingdom of Christ and live with him forever."[46]

Luther's ecclesially centered eschatology clearly links salvation with the church's sacrament of Baptism in the kingdom of Christ. It initiates a cruciform lifestyle that is grounded in the self-sacrificing passion of Jesus. Following Paul (Rom. 6:4–6), Luther correlates our being submerged and drawn out of water (Luther preferred the immersion of infants) with our eschatologically, and not merely symbolically, dying and rising with Christ.

> These two parts, being dipped under the water and emerging from it, indicate the power and effect of Baptism, which is simply the slaying of the old Adam and the resurrection of the new man, both of which must continue our whole life long. Thus a Christian life is nothing else than a

---

[44]Ibid., p. 34.
[45]Ibid., p. 448, para. 16.
[46]Ibid., p. 439, paras. 24, 25.

daily Baptism, once begun and ever continued . . . when we enter Christ's kingdom. . . .[47]

The subsequent benefits of the Lord's Supper are based on Christ's promise "for you [all]." Christ personally "nourishes and strengthens the new man" born in Baptism.[48] It is by the sacrament, "through and in which we obtain the forgiveness of sins," that Christ offers us his regenerating body and blood "as a daily food and sustenance so that our faith may refresh and strengthen itself and not weaken in the struggle, but grow continually stronger."[49]

As always, Christ intends the Word and the sacraments to be inseparable in the "kingdom of Christ." The gracious gifts of God are not to be selfishly consumed, but generously shared, as we hear, eat, and drink God's living Word as a community of saints that is being nurtured and empowered for our faithful participation in God's mission. Forgiveness and salvation have been effected in the past, offered in the present, and promised for the future. We can trust in God's sacramentally embodied Word.

> How should we know that this has been accomplished and offered to us if it were not proclaimed by preaching, by the oral Word? Whence do they know of forgiveness, and how can they grasp and appropriate it, except by steadfastly believing the Scriptures and the Gospel. Now, the whole Gospel and the article of the Creed, "I believe in the holy Christian church, the forgiveness of sins," are embodied in this sacrament and offered to us through the Word. . . .[50]

3. *Who is to receive it?* Luther concludes his discussion of Baptism by enjoining its practice for all sinful persons in general and for infants in particular. Basically, Baptism is meant for all because Christ died for all (versus the Reformed views

---

[47]Ibid., pp. 444–45, paras. 65-67.
[48]Ibid., p. 449, para. 23.
[49]Ibid., p. 449, paras. 22, 24.
[50]Ibid., p. 450, paras. 30, 32.

of God's double predestination and Christ's limited atonement). Since it is God's work and not ours, Baptism both demonstrates *sola gratia* and provides the basis for *sola fide*. "Baptism is valid, even though faith be lacking. For my faith does not constitute Baptism but receives it. . . . But it becomes beneficial to you if you accept it as God's command and ordinance, so that, baptized in the name of God, you may receive in the water the promised salvation."[51]

Luther never allows his praise of the church's Baptism to weaken his other biblical views of original sin and the life-long necessity of the benefits of Christ's cross. Baptism does not eradicate sin but rather ensures a permanent and personal relation with sin's victor, Jesus Christ, to whom we may always repentantly return for unconditional forgiveness, new life, and salvation. "Baptism remains forever . . . if anybody falls away from his Baptism, let him return to it."[52] It therefore provides us with incomparable blessings with which to withstand the devil:

> To appreciate and use Baptism aright, we must draw strength and comfort from it when our sins or conscience oppress us, and we must retort, "But I am baptized!" And if I am baptized, I have the promise that I shall be saved and have eternal life, both in soul and body.[53]

Finally, the beneficiaries of the Lord's Supper are those who faithfully trust in Christ's word of promise: "Given for you [all]" and "poured out for you [all]." Because Christ "offers and promises forgiveness of sins, it cannot be received except by faith."[54] Now since it is the strengthening of our faith by the Holy Spirit that is the very purpose of this sacramental means of grace, Luther is appalled by those so-called Lutheran Christians who now themselves abuse their

---

[51]Ibid., p. 443, para. 53; p. 441, para. 36.
[52]Ibid., p. 446, paras. 77, 85.
[53]Ibid., p. 442, para. 44.
[54]Ibid., p. 450, para. 34.

Christian freedom by "becoming listless and lazy about its observance."[55] He appeals:

> In conclusion, now that we have the right interpretation
> and doctrine of the sacrament, there is great need also of an
> admonition and entreaty that so great a treasure, which is
> daily administered and distributed among Christians, may
> not be heedlessly passed by. What I mean is that those who
> claim to be Christians should prepare themselves to receive
> this blessed sacrament frequently.
>   But suppose you say, "What if I feel that I am unfit?"
> . . . If you choose to fix your eyes on how good and pure
> you are, to work toward the time when nothing will prick
> your conscience, you will never go. . . . If you could see
> how many daggers, spears and arrows are at every
> moment aimed at you, you would be glad to come to the
> sacrament as often as possible.[56]

It was Luther's eucharistic piety in the Large Catechism that quickly served as the foundation for the reaffirmation of the validity of the purified Mass within evangelical catholic congregations in the church of the Augsburg Confession. Clearly distinguishing between the meal's frequency of administration and its personal reception, the Lutherans traditionally confessed:

> We do not abolish the Mass but religiously keep and defend
> it. In our churches, Mass is celebrated every Sunday and on
> other festivals, when the sacrament is offered to those who
> wish for it after they have been examined and absolved. We
> keep traditional liturgical forms, such as the order of the
> lessons, prayers, vestments, etc.[57]

In summary, to concentrate the church's evangelistic proclamation on its crucified and risen Lord, Luther inten-

---

[55]Ibid., p. 451, para. 40.
[56]Ibid., p. 451, para. 39; p. 453, paras. 55, 57; p. 456, para. 82.
[57]Ibid., p. 249, para. 1.

tionally revised the traditional structure of the church's classical catechism in two significant ways:

(1) he first relocated the Ten Commandments before the Creed to make Lutheranism truly "evangelical"; and

(2) he then added Holy Baptism and the Sacrament of the Altar after the Lord's Prayer to keep Lutheranism truly "catholic."

Confessional Lutherans will therefore engage in a distinctive style of evangelism in faithful obedience to these twin norms of doctrinal orthodoxy, as they are believed, taught, and confessed by God's people in the Lutheran Reformation.

CHAPTER 4

Afterword

Wıᴛʜ ᴛʜᴇ Rᴇꜰᴏʀᴍᴇʀ's ᴘʟᴇᴀ ꜰᴏʀ ᴍᴏʀᴇ ꜰʀᴇϙᴜᴇɴᴛ ꜱᴀᴄʀᴀᴍᴇɴ-
tal participation by God's Easter people still ringing in our
ears, we complete our survey of Luther's eucharistic ecclesiology in the Large Catechism. The overwhelming evidence
suggests that current Lutherans should consciously intensify
a far more churchly or communal style of evangelism. The
church, by virtue of its unique relation to the Son of God, is
called to be both a kind of "sign" and also an "instrument" of
God's inbreaking reign in the kingdom of Christ. Both its in-
reach as an "evangelical" sign and its outreach as an "evangelistic" instrument should be mutually reenforcing and
complementary. For the church's holistic mission can easily
be triumphalized without the "instrument," just as it will
likely be secularized without the "sign."

To remain an authentic expression of the communion of
saints, we need to be graciously nurtured by God's Word and
sacraments as wellsprings of the gifts of the Holy Spirit. We
will aim to "grow in grace" (2 Peter 3:18), and consider ourselves doubly blessed if we also grow in numbers. Certainly
an essential part of the church's public ministry are the incarnational practices of loving hospitality and living incultura-
tion: "The Word became flesh and lived among us" (John
1:14). We baptized and ordained priests are called to "go" to
call all others — without any exception — to participate with

us in the inclusive "mission" of God centered in our exclusive "evangelism" in Jesus Christ.

Consequently, Luther's "theology of the cross," as normed in the Large Catechism, would guide us to unite both a mission-centered view of the church (evangelical *missio Dei*) with a church-centered view of mission (catholic *missio Dei*). The same Scriptures that teach the church's "preferential option for the poor" (in ethics) also teach God's "preferential option for the church" (in mission).

It is vital to stress the uniqueness of God's mission through the church, especially in our age of cynical disillusionment with "the Establishment." There is a major loss of credibility in government, business, education, the industrial-military complex, and many other forms of institutional life. It is crucial for Christians to trust that the church is different, not because of us, but despite us and because of Christ. Though it certainly assumes an institutional character in history, the church is essentially a divine fellowship under a divine Lord. Though it looks like many other voluntary associations in society, the church alone is gathered by the Spirit and sustained by God's holy Word and sacraments. Where the church is, there is the Spirit. Though it is always in need of the continual reformation and renewal of its members, the holy church remains incomparably "the mother who bears and fosters every individual Christian" (Luther).

Only one conclusion seems to be justified from all the New Testament evidence: discipleship and churchliness are identical descriptions of the same Christ-sent reality. Those washed in Baptism and fed in Eucharist constitute the whole Christ's sent body, the church. That is, what it means to belong to Christ, as the Head of the body, is qualitatively the same as what it means to belong to the church as the body of the Head. Therefore, the best way to love Jesus is to embrace him—bodily! We must recover responsible churchliness as the current form of faithful discipleship. What the Synoptic Gospels call "discipleship" to Christ before the Crucifixion is identical with what the Pastoral Epistles describe as "churchliness" in Christ after the Resurrection.

This New Testament view of the church is desperately needed today. God wills the whole Christ's body, the church, to be sent forth as God's unique instrument for the salvation and service of humankind. To scorn the "organized" church is nothing less than heresy: ecclesiological Gnosticism! We know no other God except the God who was among us "in, with, and under" the flesh and blood of the human Jesus. So, too, we know no other kingdom of God except that which is embryonically centered in the kingdom of Christ, proleptically present "in, with, and under" the Word and sacraments of our congregations, synods, and churchwide expressions. They are at least always potentially the contemporary embodiment of God's "suffering servant" in our midst.

So long as we continue to confess our persisting sinfulness as God's redeemed saints and commit ourselves to the church's never-ending reformations, we may also boldly hold fast to our Lord's promise: "Do not be afraid, little flock, for it is your Father's good pleasure to give you the kingdom" (Luke 12:32).

In the likely troubling years ahead, we cannot avoid facing those implicit vestiges of perennial doctrinal debates that are being reenacted on current missiological soil. On the one hand, consider both the divine and human natures of Christ. After an earlier age falsely identified church missions with God's mission, a successor age has now retaliated by asserting the equally heretical separation of the two. On the other hand, consider the Holy Trinity. For some Christians to champion the salvific mission of God the Father or God the Spirit outside the church, at the expense of that which is revealed by the person and work of God the Son inside the church, is likewise false teaching. "What God has joined together, let no one separate" (Mark 10:9).

Third, consider the Holy Eucharist. In speaking of the church as a sacramental sign of salvation, is this "sign" truly an efficacious means of grace that is blessed by the whole Christ's "bodily presence" as a tangible expression of God's inbreaking reign, or is it merely a memorialized symbol of what is allegedly transpiring universally? How can the church itself now be declared an eschatological sacrament by some of those very same churches that elsewhere deny all eschatological sacraments (cf. the Lutheran-Zwinglian debate on the "real presence")?

Finally, consider eschatology. Nowhere in the New Testament are we given an exact description of the relationship between the kingdom of God and the church of Christ. The Synoptic Gospels emphasize the former before the Crucifixion; the Pastoral Epistles stress the latter after the Resurrection. Jesus Christ is God's personal link between the two; he preached the kingdom and founded the church, making the two forever inseparable but never identical.

Since Holy Scripture remains the final norm of the church's faith and life, a variety of biblical eschatologies are acceptable within the Lutheran communion, so long as they also remain decisively normed by the gospel equivalents of God's gracious justification of the ungodly in the Christ-event. So, for example, we will confessionally reject all millennialist speculations about the end of the world—especially as we approach A.D. 2000—that are based bizarrely on literalistic misinterpretations of doxological visions in the Book of Revelation (cf. the Lutheran opposition to Chiliasm).

We have seen that among the legitimate eschatologies and resultant missiologies of the New Testament, Luther's Large Catechism is most clearly indebted to Paul. In that apostolic witness considered by Luther to be "the clearest Gospel," the eschatological end (*finis*) of history is governed by its soteriological end (*telos*) at Calvary. God's raising of the crucified Jesus from the dead for us marks the definitive inauguration of God's inbreaking reign in the "new age in Christ" among us. Living "between the times" of Christ's Passion and Parousia, the church is empowered by the Holy Spirit with Word and sacrament to inaugurate God's kingdom on earth by proclaiming "Jesus Christ and him crucified" for the salvation of humankind.

At "the end"—and only at the end—testifies Paul, the Lord Christ "hands over the kingdom to God the Father, after he has destroyed every ruler and every authority and power." In the meantime, Christ's missionary church has been sent into the world as a faithful remnant to save and to serve "until he has put all his enemies under his feet" (1 Cor. 15:20-28). The decisive battle against sin and death has already been won on the cross, but the defeated enemy is not yet destroyed. In the meantime, God mandates mission!

With an eschatological realism that transcends the human alternatives of optimism and pessimism, the church militant is conscripted into the mission of the Savior against the counter-mission of Satan. It is literally an eternal death-and-life struggle that disavows all evangelistic gimmickry, razzmatazz, and triumphalistic self-adulation. May our last words also be Luther's last words: "We are truly beggars." Indeed, the blood of the martyrs will continue to be the seed of the church in every age, so long as the church's evangelistic efforts remain truly evangelical and catholic. *Soli deo gloria!*

PART II

Lutheranism: Global Mission in a Pluralistic Society

by Péri Rasolondraibe

My assignment in these pages is to comment on the following and related questions:

Does our evangelical Confessional tradition have something to contribute to evangelism? What is the relationship between confession and witness? The Confessions have been effective in protecting the gospel; do they help us proclaim the gospel effectively in a pluralistic, post-Christian, postliterate, media-dominated context? Do aspects of the Lutheran tradition inhibit evangelical outreach?

These questions are clear enough. The challenge before us is to search for and find in our Lutheran Confessional tradition some impetus to revitalize our evangelical conviction and thus to enable us to bring the gospel to bear on our present contexts. Why is this an issue for Lutheranism in America today? It is not an issue for us in Africa. Are you aware of any indications that the Evangelical Lutheran Church in America, for instance, is losing interest in or feeling awkward about evangelical outreach in the world?

Before dealing with this topic in detail, I would like to set up some parameters that will help us engage in meaningful communication.

First, let me define my perspective. I will reflect on this topic not as a professor of Confessions or of Missions, for I am not, but as a parish pastor trying to proclaim the good news of Jesus Christ through teaching and apostolic actions in an increasingly secularized and secularizing world. I approach this topic not through historical analysis of our Confessional tradition or theoretical study of Christian missions, but through the dynamic, concrete, everyday demands that pastoral ministry faces.

To be or not to be evangelical and evangelistic is the challenge I face daily in my line of witness,

• as I share the Word of God with the politically powerless and with those in the seat of power alike

• as I lead the National Council of Churches to negotiate between government, business, and the economically battered masses

• as I participated in the Malagasy national forum in the effort to put together the constitution of the third Republic of Madagascar;

• as I sit in the executive committee of the High Authority of the State during this period of transition, as its associate general secretary, and make political decisions that affect the life of the whole nation.

In my experience, when one actually reaches out into the world as Christ's disciple, one faces the temptation *not* to be evangelical and evangelistic. I will be speaking then about matters that are crucial to the church's very reason for being and relate them to our Confessional tradition.

Second, my perspective affects how I hear the question of whether Lutheranism can be both evangelical and evangelistic. The question I hear is not simply: Are we evangelical and evangelistic today? or, How can we, as evangelicals, be more evangelistic? but rather: Can we be evangelical and evangelistic in today's contexts? That is, can we be evangelical and evangelistic in a global market driven by *politique politicienne*, in a technical society where technicians fight to be the chief priests of the new world order, in a pluralistic world dominated and manipulated by the media and sustained by the spirit of *informatique*, at a time when the churches are told to accept and follow the rules of marketing in order to be competitive and thus survive in the twenty-first century?

Simply put, the question is this: When people everywhere are pushing to move beyond democracy to ethnocracy and anthropocracy, using politics and economics as means to gain power and profits, is it good news to be evangelical? Likewise, when the whole world demands marketable information, asking for the truth to be "pluriversal" and not simply universal, and when religion also converses in the language of interfaith dialogue, is it good news to be evangelistic? That is, is it good news to bring the gospel of Jesus Christ to bear on other people's lives?

CHAPTER 5

Evangelical? *Sola Gratia* in a Market-Driven Anthropocracy

WHAT DOES IT MEAN TO BE EVANGELICAL? I WOULD AGREE with the dictionary definition, namely, that *evangelical* simply means "that which is related to or in agreement with the good news of Jesus Christ." What specifically is this good news for us Lutherans? The fourth article of the Augsburg Confession has put it together for us when it says, "*[People] are freely justified for* Christ's sake through faith, when they believe that they are received into favor and that their sins *are forgiven on account of Christ, who by his death made satisfaction for our sins.*" Justification by grace alone for Christ's sake received through faith—that is the axis of our confession of faith, as it is also the converging point of our emphasis on the ministry of Word and Sacraments. This article of faith used to be the fountain of vitality for us Lutherans. Holding on to this good news makes one evangelical.

But the question today is whether this comports with the spirit of the time. Given our context, is it still good news for the world and for the church that we continue to hold on to justification by grace alone received through faith? If not, why not? As a pastor engaged in the life of a secular society, trying to bring the spirit of the gospel to bear on the political, economic arena, I find the dominant spirit of our worldwide context militating against being evangelical in the sense of *sola gratia.*

Let us find what this means by unpacking some of the major aspects of our contemporary context.

1. Economists and ecologists alike have said that one of the most basic systemic problems of our time is the assumption that unlimited economic growth is the evidence of human progress. This assumption affects politics, economics, and societal as well as natural environment, on the national, regional, and international levels.[1]

Unlimited growth is fueled by an omnipresent and highly contagious market mentality. The whole global village is transformed more and more into a gigantic shopping mall. Everything everywhere, including thought processes, personal relationships, moral values, and the worship of God, is measured by marketability. As we listen to the news from southeastern Europe, we realize that the craving for marketable commodities has taken hold of politics and the worldwide hunger for democracy has degenerated into ethnocratic tribal wars. Both of these developments reveal at their depth the surge of anthropocracy: power to the human being! The time of tutelage and ideology is over; what counts is the opportunity for human will to unfold and flourish in order to make a profit.

This surge of anthropocracy can be seen in the increasingly mass-based craving for power. Alvin Toffler a few years ago told us that at this edge of the twenty-first century, there are three sources of power in the world: knowledge, wealth, and violence. Knowledge has become the most important, since it is an invaluable capital substitute in this age of "info-wars."[2] Power to bring about whatever is humanly possible is behind the quest for knowledge, behind the hunger for wealth, and behind every maneuver of *politique politicienne*. Power for self-determination is what drives people.

One can observe this same spirit at work in the domination of the "technique," or "high tech," goddess by our so-

---

[1]Cf. Murray Bookchin, "Death of a Small Planet: It's Growth That's Killing Us" in *The Progressive* 53 (August 1989): 19-23.
[2]Cf. Alvin Toffler, *Power Shift* (New York: Bantam Books, 1990).

cietal life worldwide. A few years ago, Jacques Ellul's *Technical Society* warned us about the effect of technique on life in modern society. Actually technique has rendered life today postmodern and postliterate, artless and heartless. Here we are dealing with a spirit of neopragmatism, in which human ingenuity is measured by productivity and efficiency. "I hate mediocrity" is the password today. What is important is not so much the search for the truth or for right praxis, but simply the search for more quantity and quality of life. The spirit of high tech does not seek to revive the early twentieth-century optimism toward human achievement. It simply brings human knowledge to fruition and thus enables people to acquire profit and power.

As we reach out with the gospel of justification by grace through faith in such a context, what do we encounter? We face a forceful spirit of determination for each human being to be and to act in the world on one's own terms, to gain power through one's own achievement, to become richer and stronger, even at the expense of others. This spirit of determination to be more and better in human terms is at work not only in the world at large, but has also possessed the churches. It presents a strong challenge to the very idea of being evangelical: trusting one's life to the grace of another.

First, from both inside and outside the church we hear the criticism that certain trends in our teaching on justification by grace tend to glorify God's grace at the expense of human will. Humankind is utterly degraded in order for the victory of God's grace to be uplifted. This does not comport with the current pressure in our context to allow human ingenuity to unfold, and thus is rejected. One can frame a critique of such a view of justification from Scripture, without failing in an embrace of anthropocracy. Such a view of justification reflects a misunderstanding of God's grace to the extent that God's grace is seen in relation only to human sin and not in relation to God's love for the world and God's desire to reconcile the world to himself.

Second, there is the critique of Lutheran quietism. On the one hand, the criticism goes, Lutherans have held and practiced the belief that justification by grace is effective and is

good news for all people only if the church folds in on itself
and does not engage the life of the world in terms of its political economy or its social and natural ecology. Taught this
way, justification by grace alone reinforces people's natural
propensity for sloth when it comes to loving one's neighbor
through civic duties. It is "good news" because it gets one's
neighbor out of the way.

Quietism stems from the Lutheran dilemma about the
place of good works in the Christian life. If justification is by
grace alone, how does one talk about "faith active in love"
without falling into "faith informed by love" (*fides caritate for-
mata*)? The Majoristic controversy continues to haunt the
churches. The attempt to remove talk about good works
from the doctrine of justification, as the Formula of Concord
did in 1580, did not solve our problem in the long run. Instead it has impelled Lutherans into maintenance ministry.

On the other hand, the critique of Lutheran quietism continues; the doctrine of good works in the Lutheran Confessional writings is set in the context of the "two-regiments
doctrine." Lutheran churches believe they can be "evangelical" and engage in the life of their world as long as they
maintain a proper distinction between the two spheres in
which God exercises sovereignty. The two-regiments doctrine recognizes the rule of God through law and justice over
all human endeavor in the kingdom on the left. It under-
stands the evangelical rule of Christ to prevail primarily in
the realm of faith in the kingdom on the right and to impinge
on the kingdoms of this world only through the witness of
individual Christians. According to this doctrine, the church
engages in the life of the world only indirectly through her
members posted in different stations of secular life. What the
church can or should do is encourage its members to be faithful in their callings.

Critics observe, however, that being evangelical only
through indirect participation is not effective in bringing
about needed changes. More often than not, individual
Christians are easily co-opted by the dominant spirit of their
context. "New wine must be put in new wineskins." If the
church does not engage the life of the world directly and res-

olutely, sinful structures will corrupt Christian witnesses. Furthermore, ethics based on the First Article of the Creed alone, without the sustaining power of the Second and Third Articles, cannot give strong moorings to Christian witness, but rather degenerates quickly into natural law. There may be danger of triumphalism in a Christian integrist approach to social/political life. A Lutheran laissez-faire social ethics, however, is even more dangerous.

Luther taught not only about the two regiments through which God rules, but also about two kingdoms at war with each other, namely, the kingdom of God and the kingdom of Satan. The focus of the battle of God's kingdom against that of Satan is christological; and this christological background must be brought to bear on the working of the two regiments. This reminder of Luther's two-kingdoms doctrine calls for a dynamic understanding of justification by grace as over against a static understanding of justification. We will come back to that later.

Third, there is criticism that the Lutheran understanding of justification focuses on the believer's attention on otherworldly concerns and promotes dependency. In the political arena, justification by grace is looked upon as politically suspect, as an ideological distraction meant to divert people's interest and energy from the reality of their struggle for self-determination. The African Methodist theologian Gabriel Setiloane of Botswana University once wrote that, in his opinion, the Roman Catholic teaching on justification, which takes seriously the care for this life, is far better than the Protestant one for Africa as a developing continent. Africans, in his view, should fight dependency mentality both in the political economy and in religious matters, for the one feeds into the other. Does justification by grace alone teach dependency or a beggar mentality? If that were true, then the whole discussion about collaboration between colonialism and mission would take on another dimension.

Fourth, there is criticism of practice. Questions are raised about the way some churches live out their evangelical identity. *Sola gratia* informs many teachings of the Lutheran churches. But does it inform their actions? Many churches in the northwest today believe the forecasters who say that in order for churches to be in business in the year 2000, they must learn to attract and keep people by using telemarketing techniques.[3] "A church that cannot sell itself is going to lose out to the competition." Churches that act on these marketing principles become self-centered. Efficient church management and organizational success become more important than the power of the Word of God that transforms people's lives and turns the church inside out.

Today we Christians who come from the project-submitting and scholarship-begging churches suffer greatly at the hands of arrogant technocrats in the materially wealthy churches, as the spirit of profitability and not that of *sola gratia* guides their decisions. The church borrows from the world more than it is able to give to the world. Even from within the life experience of the Lutheran churches, being evangelical, to the extent that what is taught is different from what is enacted, is not good news.

Where do we go from here? We meet anthropocracy at every turn. It would seem that we can hold on to justification *sola gratia* only in our proverbial ecclesiastical closet. When we ask, "Lutheranism: Evangelical?" the answer is already given. As children of the Reformation, we hold on to the good news of Jesus Christ, come what may. We are Protestants! We believe and have come to know that this good news is life for the world. The question, therefore, is how do we repossess this good news so that we will be free from the spirit of the world that has possessed us and prevented us from being evangelical in the life of the world?

Dynamic Justification

I propose that we consider repenting from our tendency to glory in a religion of remembrance, that is, a religion that focuses on the past, rehearsing it in such a way that it fosters an

---

[3]John Naisbitt and Patricia Aburdene, *Megatrends 2000* (New York: William Morrow and Company Inc., 1990), 290-91.

ideological hope for the future. By focusing on the past we avoid facing the traumas, injustices, and needs of the present. This is the situation that Jesus encountered in the temple religion of his time. It was a religion that facilitated the smooth running of the dominant culture. It was a religion that was successful in removing itself from the present and locking itself in the past so that people's day-to-day life was safe from God. God was placated and kept outside of human life so that human beings could do what they wished to do with each other. This is the temple of which Jesus said, "Destroy this temple and I will raise it again in three days."

We Lutherans must take a hard look at the basis of our teaching and the shape of our ministry so as not to fall into the trap of becoming a religion of remembrance. This need is more acute for Lutherans in the West or North Atlantic countries because Western people are culturally time based as opposed to space based. Translated into Christian terms, this means that Western Christians express their spirituality through the medium of time, in terms of remembrance and hope, past and eternity. But to meet the challenge of our global context, which has moved beyond time-based concepts, we must return to the dynamic biblical approach to justification. The biblical approach is dynamic in the sense that it puts forward God's *dynamis* (power), which creates meaning, purpose, direction, movement, and empowerment for us.

Biblical witnesses (Pauline, Johannine, Lukan) agree that our justification is not simply *from* something but also *for* something. When we wonder what justifies our occupying a space in this universe, we are inquiring about purpose and meaning. I can find justification for some of the things I do or maybe even the totality of my acts, but I cannot find justification for my being in this world that cannot justify even its own existence. The apostle Paul gives us insight into dynamic justification in Romans, as he does in Ephesians:

> We know that in everything God works for good with those who love him, who are called according to his purpose. For those whom he foreknew he also predestined to

> be conformed to the image of his Son. . . . And those
> whom he predestined he also called; and those whom he
> called he also justified; and those whom he justified he also
> glorified. (Rom. 8:28-30, RSV)

According to Paul, the only one who holds the justification for our being in this world is God. Paul says in Ephesians 1 that God, before the foundation of the world, has placed us in the history of Jesus Christ, to be conformed to the image of his Son, to be given to the world with Christ. Justification *sola gratia* means this: God has given us the invitation, the permission, and thus the empowerment to be co-heirs with Christ, both of his suffering and of his glory.

Justification *sola gratia* is justification for mission in and to the world. *Sola gratia* does not keep the church away from the world but instead sends the church in the midst of a market-driven anthropocracy to "event" the good news within it. To be evangelical does not mean simply to hold on to the proclamation of the good news but also to bring about the good news wherever the church is. For the church to be good news in this global market where cash, convenience, and consumerism reign, it must know that it has its origin in the fullness of God's grace and not in the emptiness of a power-hungry world. The church is not competing with the world in order to fill its cup with the dregs of the world. Rather it is appointed by grace to empty itself in the world, to "enrich" the world. For the church to enrich the world requires that it not swim with the tide of market mentality, pursue the drive for power, or adopt a technique-worshiping lifestyle. It requires that the church be the instrument of God's dynamic grace in the world poured out so that grace-filled life unfolds for the world. This is what being evangelical means.

Costly Grace

But isn't this too costly for us individually and for the church as a whole? Yes, it is costly. To echo Bonhoeffer's powerful insight, grace is never cheap; it is always costly for God and for those whom God has elected in Jesus Christ to be heirs of

God's kingdom. It is costly, and that is why it is good news for the world. When God gives something, it is the best. Paul describes this costly grace, this dynamic justification:

> But we have this treasure in earthen vessels, to show that the transcendent power belongs to God and not to us. We are afflicted in every way, but not crushed; perplexed, but not driven to despair; persecuted, but not forsaken; struck down, but not destroyed; always carrying in the body the death of Jesus, so that the life of Jesus may also be manifested in our bodies. For while we live we are always being given up to death for Jesus' sake, so that the life of Jesus may be manifested in our mortal flesh. So death is at work in us, but life in you. (2 Cor. 4:7-12, RSV)

For us to be evangelical is good news for the world. As the church empties itself in the world, God's grace works healing in the world as salt and light. This I know for a fact, having experienced in the last two years the churches in Madagascar emptying themselves by standing with the poverty-stricken masses when they call for structural changes. The churches and their leaders became objects of repression, criticism, and ridicule. But the corrupt structures were changed, and the people were given new hope.

We turn next to the Confessional basis of the church's evangelistic outreach and the problems we now face in being evangelistic in today's world.

CHAPTER 6

Evangelistic? *Sola Scriptura* in a Media-Dominated Pluralistic Society

W E HAVE SEEN THAT BEING EVANGELICAL GOES AGAINST THE grain of the dominant spirit of our time, namely, the search and struggle for anthropocracy in all spheres of life. Our calling, however, is not to be anything but evangelical. It is to swim against the tide and reexamine our understanding of what it means to be evangelical. Also, we must have a dynamic understanding of justification by grace. This justification is "dynamic" because we are not simply rehearsing the past but are led into new life, which is the purpose of justification. This justification is "by grace" because our being and acting in the world is justified on the basis of God's gracious invitation, permission, and therefore empowerment for us to be God's salt and light, God's sacramental elements of love for the healing of this broken world.

Our concern in this chapter is about being evangelistic in our present context. We shall inquire whether our evangelical Confessional tradition has something to contribute to evangelism and whether the Confessions help us proclaim the gospel effectively in a pluralistic, post-Christian, postliterate, media-dominated context. We will deal with the first question in this chapter and with the second, namely, effectiveness in proclaiming the gospel, in the next.

First, we need to be clear about what we mean by the evangelical Confessional tradition. On the one hand, it can refer to a body of Confessional writings regarded as authoritative in matters of doctrine and action by succeeding generations of specific Christian groups. In the case of Western Lutheranism, it could be that body of Confessional writings compiled in *The Book of Concord*. On the other hand, one can also look at the Confessional tradition, like any tradition, not as a locked text but as an ongoing open text, always in the making, always being written and rewritten.

As we look at our Confessional writings, the locked texts that we inherited, we realize very quickly that evangelism, in the sense of sharing the gospel of Jesus Christ with those who have not heard it, was not the priority of the struggling, nascent evangelical church. What was important for the Reformers, both theologians and princes, was to protect the purity of doctrine, especially the doctrine of justification by grace through faith in Jesus Christ, for the sake of the frightened conscience of people, those within Christendom.

Pagans and Gentiles are mentioned occasionally in these writings, primarily as examples of idolatrous, faithless, self-righteous, ungodly people, whose religions fell in the same category as those of the Pharisees and the "papists." The Turks were the closest "heathen" known to the Reformers, but they were looked upon not as potential recipients of God's justifying grace through the ministry of the church but rather as enemies of Christendom. Driving them out of the country by force would constitute a good work for the emperor (Augsburg Confession 21.1).

Sharing the faith among the laity within Christendom was a rare thing, perhaps because of the deplorable ignorance of the people (cf. Luther's preface to the Small Catechism). Lay evangelism is not mentioned at all in these writings, except in the Smalcald Articles, where Luther talks about the gospel "which offers counsel and help against sin . . . through the mutual conversation and consolation of brethren" (S.A. 4). These Brethren here may very well be pastors and theologians talking to each other, but it is possible that these were lay people sharing the gospel among themselves. So there is here a hint of lay evangelism.

Evangelism, in the sense of evangelistic outreach, can also refer to the effort of the church to bring the good news of

Jesus Christ to bear on the life of society as a whole through the good works of its members. Our Confessional writings discuss at great length the good works that the children of God do in private as well as in public life, depending on their callings. As we read these Confessional writings, we are aware of two important determining factors about the nature of those good works.

First, they must be seen through the lens of the frightened conscience searching for a merciful God and needing assurance of its own salvation. Thus, though good works must flow from a living faith, they must never be confused with justification. Doing good works does not necessarily tie in with being evangelical.

Second, good works must be seen through the lens of a struggling, threatened, battered church, trying to avoid provoking or alienating the state so that it can survive and consolidate its acquisitions. Thus, good works must not be threatening to the established powers. Good works, performed either by the individual Christian or by the church as a whole, must help maintain the good order of the state. Does that assume that the state will always be at the service of Christendom? We know that when Christendom collapsed and the church once again faced an unfriendly world with its corrupt and totalitarian governments, Christian witness in the world was radically changed.

Without being judgmental toward the authors of these writings, I wonder, given the many constraints that informed their theological presuppositions, whether they have much help to give us in our effort to understand how to be evangelical and evangelistic in our complex context today.

But the Confessional tradition is not only authoritative books from the past; it is also a tradition in the making. Our call to witness challenges us to unlock the Confessional writings, to free ourselves of the hold of Lutheran orthodoxy and scholasticism as the Pietists did in their time, and to go directly to the power that underlies the evangelical Confessional tradition, namely, the Word of God. Our Confessional writings make it very clear that the Word of God, both proclaimed and visible (the sacraments), is the foundation and cornerstone of the being of the church and its ministry (Augsburg Confession 5 and 7). I believe that here we have the theological basis we need to talk about being evangelical and evangelistic.

As we unlock the Confessional writings in order to join the ongoing tradition, we need to rethink our understanding of the ministry of Word and Sacraments. We need to relate it not only to the doctrine of justification, as the Confessions do, but also to the doctrine of the Trinity and to the understanding of the Word as *dabar* (a creative and generative word). I understand that it is no longer within the reach of most Western people to experience the *word* as creating what it stands for. But the inability to experience its generative power does not make the Word of God less generative. It is still what Isaiah heard it to be:

> For as the rain and the snow come down from heaven,
> and return not thither but water the earth,
> making it bring forth and sprout,
> giving seed to the sower and bread to the eater,
> so shall my word be that goes forth from my mouth;
> it shall not return to me empty,
> but it shall accomplish that which I purpose,
> and prosper in the thing for which I sent it.
> (Isa. 55:10-11)

Ministry in the Light of Trinitarian Christology

WE TRADITIONALLY TALK ABOUT THE TRINITY AS A COMMUNITY of life and love. Three interlocked divine entities are dwelling in each other in eternal self-givingness and mutual empowerment, not out of need or necessity, but out of the abundance and freedom of divine love. Through the history of this triune love in relation to us, however, we learn to know that God is also a community of divine sentness: The Father and the Spirit send the Son to redeem the world; the Father and the Son send the Spirit to regenerate the world; and the Son and the Spirit offer the Father so that the world might be reconciled to God, calling God "Abba, Father." As we walk alongside of the biblical community, we learn to appreciate the fact that this triune *God is an eccentric God*, a God whose center of interest is outside the Godself. This is a God who tears the Godself apart, as it were, in order to give away what God cherishes the most for the well-being of that which is other than God, even against God, namely, the world. Furthermore, as we are brought into the history of this eccentric God through baptism, we come to understand that God's "I love you" coincides with God's "I am sending you to the world." There are no saints who are not sent!

Ministry in the Light of the Word as *Dabar*

THE MINISTRY OF THE CHURCH, THE MINISTRY OF WORD AND Sacraments, is derived from the history of this eccentric God with us. Our understanding of the Word, in the light of our sentness, leads us to move away from viewing the Word as merely declarative or enunciative. That would reduce it to mere verbalism (cf. Paul Freire). The Word that created and recreates the church is generative in the sense that it evokes, generates, makes concrete, "events" what it stands for. As Paul put it: "God is able to do what God promises." In biblical terms, the Word is light and life (*zōē* Rom. 4:21). Life, as the Greek *zōē* indicates, is a divine (Trinitarian) quality of life. It is life laid down for another (John 15:13). It is a body broken and blood poured out for others (cf. Christ's last supper).

So it is with regard to ministry. The Word as light, like light in the story of creation, removes our darkness as it judges it and that of our world and generates in us and in the world the space and time for life to unfold. The light that the Word generates does not simply provide us with a religious enlightenment, it initiates the destruction of what we hold secure, so that there may be space and time for a creature of faith and love, a child of God, to be and to act.

Thus, on the one hand, the Word as Light generates the death process of the sinful, egocentric self, while generating the birth process of a life-giving sacramental self. On the other hand, the Word as life (*zōē*, life poured out for others) is the light or orientation for existence in this world created by and for the Word. In other words, the Word is the light of our existence, and that light is determined by the Trinitarian quality of life. The ministry of the Word, therefore, is not simply a declarative action (maintenance ministry). It is a dynamic, creative, God-at-work ministry.

Furthermore, the sacraments as "visible words" and generative events, generate sacramental selves in the world. Baptism initiates the transformation of sacrificial self into sacramental self. For in baptism, God, as a community of sentness, receives the offered self by offering it back to the world as an instrument of God's righteousness. The believer's reception into God's kingdom *is* being sent into the world. In biblical terms, it is as we die in baptism that the world can really have us as gifts of God's grace. Without this Word creating this space for God's sacramental selves, we are bad news for the world.

Likewise, the Lord's Supper is the actualization of our "re-membering" with the Lord ("Do this in remembrance of me"). As we share in the life of Christ (re-membered with him), and thus become members of one another, we are empowered to become sacramental elements of divine life to the world. These generative events, therefore, are sacraments of God's gracious invitation, permission, and empowerment for us to be the salt and light of the world: to bring life where death seems to have the final word, to bring hope where dead-end thinking has set in, to fight for justice where oppression is part of normalcy, to educate for peace even where it is believed to be economically more profitable to prepare for war.

Our ongoing Confessional tradition teaches us that to be evangelical, that is, to hold on to the good news of Jesus Christ, unfolds itself in being evangelistic, that is, to "event" the good news of Jesus Christ in the here and now. One comes with the other, as the one is glorified in the other.

But how can this rereading of tradition help us engage in evangelistic outreach in a pluralistic, post-Christian, media-dominated context? When we talk about evangelistic outreach, we need to distinguish it from evangelical outreach. Evangelical outreach is used by some to refer particularly to social services provided by churches, such as disaster relief, refugee assistance, and various development projects, without specific reference to the good news of Jesus Christ. Neither the world nor the churches have a problem with such evangelical outreach, understood as a humanitarian gesture with no strings attached. The problem we face is with evangelistic outreach, that is, with the churches' reaching out in word and deed into the world with the life transforming good news of Jesus Christ.

Let us be honest with ourselves. Where does our problem with evangelistic outreach lie? Does it lie primarily in a changing context or in a changing church?

It is fair to say, without exaggeration, that the beginning of the 1970s already witnessed a waning of the Western churches' zeal for mission, both global and local. Giving for mission outreach decreased; lifetime commitment for missionary endeavor diminished; funding for mission projects was being phased out. There has been a growing feeling of uneasiness concerning talk about evangelization, especially when one clearly says that to evangelize means to bring people to Christ. We still find it difficult in Western Lutheranism to talk meaningfully about bringing the gospel to bear on the life of the society beyond the church.

There has been a weakening of our conviction that evangelization (evangelistic outreach) is central to the church's reason for being. Moreover, individualism has deeply informed our theologies and church practices in the West to the extent that faith has receded into the closet of private life and Christians find it difficult or even inappropriate to share their faith with others. Why is there this weakening of our convictions about evangelization? Where does the problem lie? There are various reasons. Let us begin with the external factors.

We must recognize, to begin with, that our present global context is not fertile ground for evangelization. This is not new or peculiar to this end of the twentieth century. Throughout the ages, Christian evangelistic outreach has always encountered resistance from the world. Persecution and martyrdom are familiar biblical terms for Christians who take seriously their being sent into the world. Nevertheless, we need to understand the particularity of the challenges we face in our present context in order to think more constructively about effectiveness in evangelization.

First, there is an increasingly globalized call for pluralism. In many places the call for pluralism seems to be riding on the tide of democratic reform. Religious pluralism is not a new phenomenon. It can be helpful to the church when Christianity is in a minority position. Today, however, we are dealing with people who do not simply say that there are plural ways to God or to whatever stands for ultimate reality, but who say that reality itself, the truth, is not necessarily one, but may itself be plural. In religious circles, this form of pluralism leads to a functional view of religion. As long as a religion makes people's lives more enjoyable and socially harmonious, then it is good and should not be disturbed by other religions. All claims for finality by particular worldviews, political ideologies, philosophies, or religions are called into question. Wisdom, enlightened by the spirit of profitability, dictates that all search for truth should be allowed to flourish so that the world gains a richer, fuller experience of whatever there is to be had. In this sense, pluralism stands as a challenge to evangelization. If Christianity represents only a tiny spark of what can be experienced, why should it be allowed to impose its parochial view on the rest of the world?

Alongside of this view of pluralism and feeding on it is the media explosion, which renders the peddling of old stories a bore and economically self-defeating. Like the Athenians of old, people are hungry for new things to experience or from which to make a profit.

In addition, we must say something about interfaith dialogue. Such dialogue has achieved some degree of success in increasing religious tolerance in the world through mutual understanding and respect. This success has been misunderstood in some Christian circles to signal the fading away of

Christian witness in the world. Meanwhile, Muslims are using their petro-dollars to win the whole world for Allah. Second, being careful not to confuse or collapse evangelical outreach with global mission, we must mention briefly some long-standing criticisms against evangelization, especially in the form of cross-cultural mission.

Objections from Religion

Do Christians claim to be the only ones who possess divine revelation, namely, through Jesus Christ? The question we face is this: Given the freedom of God, how do we relate faith in Jesus Christ to the possibility of divine revelation in other religions? Can one really say that God is not known as a merciful God in places where Christ is not known?

Many Christians feel relieved by this emphasis on general revelation. If God is somehow at work through many religions, then we do not have to torture our consciences about those who do not know Christ. Some theologians are quite willing to drop the filioque clause from the Nicene Creed, with the understanding that the Holy Spirit should be free to operate in the world without Christ. The Holy Spirit will cover for us.

Objections from Culture

Western Christianity, whether coming directly from the West or by way of former mission fields, destroys other people's cultures by imposing its mores and cultural values on them. From the people of the two-thirds world, this is a double-pronged criticism. On the one hand, they claim that cultural renaissance is one way for peripheral countries to fight dependency. Asians and Africans, at home or in the diaspora, and Native Americans, both North and South, are saying that it is necessary for their survival in the face of the onslaught of Western influence that they keep and strengthen their cultures. Western Christianity as a civilization militates against this cultural renaissance and thus must be rejected. On the other hand, they say that "the gospel is not Western." They claim that Western culture has distorted the gospel so much that if one wishes to hear the good news, one has to go to the biblical roots and move directly into one's culture. No help from the West is needed.

I personally have heard Lutheran pastors in the West use this argument many times. They say, "You don't need us; you have the Bible!" What I always say is, "How about you? Do you need us now that you have the Bible?" What is a church without mission?

In addition, anthropologists (mostly Western) bemoan the fact that traditional ways of life in Asia, Africa, and the Americas are fast disappearing because of the onslaught of Western culture, facilitated by the spread of Western Christianity. What, one may ask, is the motivation behind such concern for traditional ways of life? Is it care for the people of Asia, Africa, and the Americas?

Objections from Political Ideology

Why should Western Christianity be allowed to inculcate Western imperialist ideologies on people? In the West the privatization of faith gives free rein for the invisible hand of the market economy to shape the public lives of people, both national and international. In the South, Christianity came with the expansion of Western imperialism (mercantilism, colonialism, and neocolonialism) and has directly or indirectly facilitated it. Both in the Northwest and in the South, Western Christianity, operating as a political ideology, has helped a rich minority gain control over the global economy while pushing the poor majority to the periphery.

People in peripheral countries (especially the elite) are asking themselves, Why should we remain in this religion of our slave masters? Why should we embrace a religion that seems to favor a powerful racist minority? One wonders why the waning of missionary zeal coincided with the political independence of the mission fields.

Objections from Environmentalists

The environmentalists say that the imperialistic, androcentric drive underlying the Judeo-Christian belief system has been detrimental to survival on this planet. First, the view that humankind is to have domination (not only dominion) over creation has brought destruction to the natural environment. Second, the emphasis on redemption (over against creation) works against care for creation. The new creation does away with the old. Since this criticism was first heard, the church has come a long way toward saving the environment, both theologically and in practice. But the thrust of this criticism aims at the heart of Christianity itself, namely, our faith in redemption, new creation.

These are serious criticisms and even indictments. They should not be taken lightly. Some of them have actually paralyzed mission societies into giving up global mission work in some parts of the world. They have also discouraged churches from engaging in evangelistic outreach at home. Be that as it may, I do not think that they should be allowed to change the good news for us. The good news says that when we are received by God through grace we are also sent into the world as sacramental selves, as salt and light. For this good news is not some ideology of our own making. It comes as God's gift to us. "You are a chosen race, a royal priesthood, a holy nation, God's own people, that you may declare the wonderful deeds of him who called you out of darkness into his marvelous light" (1 Peter 2:9-10).

The world may opt for pluralism, but that does not mean that we have lost our voice and our share of experience in such a world. Religious, cultural, political, and environmental concerns are not really threats to evangelistic outreach but to a certain brand of otherworldly evangelism. Whenever the good news of our gift-ness to the world is carefully and abundantly translated into life-giving and transforming actions, churches are called upon to heal societal and national crises. Being evangelical, that is, holding on to the good news of Jesus Christ, it is our calling through the gospel to be evangelistic, that is, to actualize the good news in people's lives. As liberation theologians used to say, to know Christ is to follow him.

How can we regain the conviction that being evangelical and evangelistic are tied together? We must first regain the centrality of the Word of God in the life and ministry of the church. We must shake ourselves free from the hold of dogmatics and the spirit of scholasticism on us, and learn from the biblical community what it means to be "pregnant with the Word." The apostle Paul was able to face the pluralistic Athenian society and to preach Christ and his resurrection to them, because he did not come to them empty-handed; he came "pregnant with the Word." We must go back to the study of Scripture, not as tourists looking for novelty, but as children of God who thirst for the Word of life. It is through constant, in-depth study of the Scripture that Christians get to know Christ and thus are empowered by the Spirit to follow him, to walk the way of the Son. Paul knew this well when he urged the Colossians, "Let the word of Christ dwell in you richly" (Col. 3:16). Someone has said, "If you have Christ, you cannot hide him." Flood a congregation with the study of the Word of God and they will not ask what it means to be evangelistic. It is here that we need to understand and know the Word as creative and generative event. The Word does something to the hearer.

The problem with many churches today is that they are led not by blind leaders but by leaders who are deaf to the Word of God, who replace the Word with platitudes. In many churches today genuine love for the Word of God is unknown. Many pastors do not have the will, the time, nor the ability to study the Scriptures with people.

And so, does our Confessional tradition have something to contribute to evangelism? The answer is yes: *sola scriptura!* The centrality of the Word is the answer. The Word authorizes and empowers us to be and to act as God's children in God's world. As a parish pastor who deals daily with the problem of evangelistic outreach, I can say with all confidence that only churches who feed constantly on the Word of God can be evangelistic in this so-called post-Christian, postliterate world.

CHAPTER 7

Confessional and Confessing? Faith-ing the *Sola Fide*

ALTHOUGH IT IS A GREAT TEMPTATION FOR US TO BE OTHER than evangelical and although the world is not always a fertile ground for evangelization, we cannot be other than what God has chosen us to be, namely, "God's own people, that [we] may declare the wonderful deeds of him who called [us] out of darkness into his marvelous light" (1 Peter 2:9). In this chapter we turn to the mode and shape of evangelistic outreach in some detail. More specifically, we will try to unpack what we mean when we say to know Christ is to follow him. More specifically, we will raise the question, Do we belong to a confession in the sense of being owned by it and limited to it, or do we actualize what we confess in the sense of being freed and empowered by it to act? I see the church not as an organization defined and bound together by a body of Confessional writings, but as a gathering of believers who hear and respond to Christ's call to follow (cf. Augsburg Confession, 5). The authority of the Confessions, for me, resides not in our regarding them as binding, limiting, and paralyzing but rather in the fact that they liberate, authorize, and enable the church to follow Christ.

Another caveat: Justification by grace is the starting-point of our evangelistic outreach and not the point we wish to attain. Forgiveness of sins is not the crowning of our own efforts; it is the gift of God's mercy. Yet at the same time the forgiveness of sins is also the sending of the sinner into the world to follow Christ. Forgiveness of sins enables one to pick up one's cross and follow Christ and not simply to sit at the foot of the cross. Justification is liberation from the bondage of sin as well as empowerment to be God's sacramental elements of love in the world. We will say more later about the forgiveness of sins as it is translated into concrete actions in society. We need to be clear about this starting point so that when we begin to talk about outreach all thought of works righteousness will be exorcised from our midst. At the same time any thought of spectator or consumer theology is also thrown out the window.

To Know Christ Is to Follow Christ

WHEN WE CONFESS THAT THE VERY BEING OF THE CHURCH AND of every individual member of the church comes from the generative Word of God, we are also saying that the reason for our being in the world is hidden in Christ's call to us to follow him, that is, in his generative Word to us. Christ's call, "You, follow me!" was not addressed only to Peter and Levi; it is addressed also to us. The question is: Where do we follow Christ?

We Follow Christ as Individual Christians

Like most ethicists who follow the example of Luther and Calvin, I agree that we as individual Christians follow Christ in the four spheres of life: the family (domestic relations), the society (social relations), the place of work (economic relations), and the state (political relations). These are structures of human relations that exist today, but they are not the only possible ones. Other theologians talk about five spheres: family, work, society, nation, and world.

The Lutheran tradition insists that we follow Christ in these spheres of life, because we believe that the good news consists not in our getting out of the world (monastic life) but in our being sent into the world to care for the world. In our present context we hear the call to follow Christ in and through these spheres of life.

The family sphere is the initial and also the continuing place where we are called to be sacramental selves. The call comes to the Christian as a father, for instance, but it also comes to the same person as a husband, a brother, an uncle, a son, and so on. The call comes with and through the different opportunities one encounters in the family sphere. Christ does not come to us alone (Bonhoeffer); he brings guests with him and then calls us to follow him. The Christian person responds to the call not simply according to the established rules of social morality as, for example, a father, a husband, or a brother is expected to respond, but as following Christ authorizes him/her to respond. The Christian must learn anew in each situation what it means to follow Christ as a father or a son or a husband. Following Christ within the domestic sphere is the most difficult and trying experience for a Christian, because one meets the call at every turn and one cannot walk away from it.

In the sphere of social relations, the call comes to the Christian as neighbor. Evangelistic outreach takes on its first public shape in the call to make living together possible. One hears the call to follow Christ in and through the needs of the neighbor and the neighborhood. Such needs do not come as problems or social cases to be solved but as opportunities to create space and time for life to unfold. When needs arise that usually are referred to as social problems (crime, drugs, delinquency, perversions, homelessness, public health crises, and such), that is a sign that calls have gone unheeded, that along the way we did not hear or respond to the call to follow.

One very important way Christians respond to the call in the social sphere is by sharing the good news of Jesus Christ. Christians share the gospel individually or as part of a group, such as family cells, town sections, or base communities. In many parts of the world, Christians are reaching out in the community as the arm of the church at work seven days a week through door-to-door evangelism, Bible study sessions, caring for the sick and elderly, and welcoming newcomers.

In the sphere of our place of work (our profession), we recognize that there are different levels of callings.

1. In our professional calling, we follow Christ by doing well what we do best. Whatever our profession may be, our work is aimed at contributing to the well-being of society and the nation as a whole. Our Confessional writings make this point clear.

2. In the sphere of our work Christians are also called to care socially and spiritually for co-workers as we share in their lives and their problems. It has become a widespread custom in Madagascar and in other parts of Africa for Christian workers to hold prayer meetings and counseling sessions at their place of work outside of their working hours. Such services respond to the felt needs of their co-workers.

3. But our calling in the economic sphere does not end there. Workers who follow Christ are always confronted with the call to be conscious of the consequences their line of work has on their community, the environment, their nation's economy, and the well-being of the whole world. As a parish pastor, I counseled industrial workers and government officials who faced difficulties in their jobs because they dared to challenge the policies of their workplace or to oppose the position of their labor union. When I asked why they were willing to risk their careers, they answered: "We feel called to do so and would not do otherwise!"

The Christian worker's calling is to provide a strong and healthy national economy, but at the same time to be the salt and light of his or her workplace, not allowing Adam Smith's hidden hand alone to shape human relations in the economic sphere.

In the sphere of the state or of political relations every Christian is called to follow Christ as a citizen. Christians are free to join political parties but must prayerfully watch that they do not become co-opted by the *politique politicienne* of special interests. Furthermore, as our Confessional writings said very forcefully, Christians are free to assume responsibilities in government and in all state business locally, nationally, and internationally. In whatever position Christians are called to serve, they are also called to stand against all forms of corruption and abuse of power. For Christians are called not only to work under and abide by the law of the land, they are called also to be lawmakers. Here the transforming nature of Christian outreach takes on primary importance.

We Follow Christ as a Church

Whether we like it or not, the church as an organized institution is a political entity which, depending on the circumstances, has more or less political clout. The church cannot crawl under its steeples and say that it has nothing to do with life outside the church. The church is not a monastery or a sanctuary where one can run away from the world. For the church of today to hope to stand on neutral ground politically is already a political stand. It is the worst kind of political stand because it endorses without any reservation the powers that be.

Christ's call to follow him comes not only to individual Christians, but also to the church as a community of believers. What does it mean for the church to follow Christ? The primary calling of the church is to proclaim God's generative Word, which is the light and life of the world. How does the church go about doing that?

Church and Politics. Although the church is an organized institution with political clout, it is not a political party, does not act like a political party, and does not join or support one particular political party. Political parties are based on group interests, each trying to shift the balance of political and economic power to their advantage. Because the various group interests are represented in the church, the church cannot take sides without alienating part of the body. The church, however, is called on all occasions to address political situations while proclaiming the Word as light and life.

Church and State. Our Confessional writings look upon the state mainly as God's instrument of justice to curb and punish sin. This is a limited view. The state should also be seen as God's instrument of life and peace to protect human life and to enhance the quality of life for all people.

The church's evangelistic outreach in the sphere of the state takes shape in its proclaiming the Word as light. It raises a prophetic voice and brings judgment on all sinful political economic acts and structures. To bring the life of the state into the light of the Word of God cannot be done lightly or hastily. It has to be done prayerfully and with firm resolution. The Word as light aims to create space and time for life to unfold. When the church proclaims this Word, it unmasks and judges sinful situations and thereby provides a space for individual Christians to act out their callings more effectively. For as we know, Christians may do their best according to their calling, but if corrupt and sinful structures are left unchallenged, their good works simply reinforce corruption in public life.

Carrying out this ministry of the Word as light is a dangerous calling for the church, for it is always met with repression by the powers that be. We must know, however, not only that we respond to a call that is stronger than our fear of danger, but also that this ministry of prophesying against the sinful structures of the commanding heights brings hope and empowerment to the individual Christians who are caught up and languish within those structures. Churches located in internationally powerful countries should heed the call to prophesy for the well-being of the whole international community.

Church and Society. The ministry of the church is also to proclaim the Word as life — life for the state through life in the community. As our Confessional writings rightly state, the primary work of the church is the proclamation of forgiveness of sins for Christ's sake. This is the ministry of the Word as life, for it releases the guilty conscience from its bondage and sets it free to live the life of a child of God. When we talk about forgiveness of sins we need to remind ourselves that sin has two consequences, guilt and shame. We usually tend to overemphasize the guilt without addressing the shame. Guilt is psychological and spiritual while shame is social and spatial. Guilt is removed when the offended person forgives the repentant offender. Shame continues to haunt the life of both the offender and the offended until the cause of social and spatial disruption is removed and reconciling harmony is restored. Evangelistic outreach to society through the proclamation of forgiveness of sins must take into account the shame that human sinfulness brings into the life of the community. The Word of life removes shame and generates healing through visible concrete actions of the church.

Moreover, the ministry of the Word as life goes beyond the "eventing" of forgiveness of sins. It generates the courage to be human and the hope to live for God. In evangelical outreach to society, as the church brings the Word of life close to the lives of people, it is called to make life unfold. It must not only preach eternal life, but also feed the hungry with food; not only preach spiritual well-being, but heal the sick; not only preach release to the captives, but bring hope and dignity to the prisoners.

For the church to prophesy the unfolding of life through proclamation and apostolic actions does not mean that it relieves the state of its social responsibilities. Rather, the church points the direction for the state to follow. It does not mean that the church indulges in tokenism, as it is always accused of doing when it becomes socially involved. It means that in the course of following Christ, its footprints clearly indicate where life is unfolding.

The Way of Filiation

AS WE HEAR THE CALL TO FOLLOW CHRIST, HOW DO WE KNOW what to do? As I hear the call to follow Christ, what am I to do? Some theologians (the Barthian camp) tell us that if it is really Christ's call that we hear, then we will also hear what we are commanded to do, because God's invitation to act is also God's permission and command. This may be true in the case of the individual, but it is difficult for the whole church to hear Christ's call as a guide to action. Other theologians (the *Koinonia* camp) tell us to come together as a fellowship (koinonia) in the church (*ecclesiola in ecclesia*) and find what we are to do through prayer and the reading of Scripture. I think this is helpful; but for the church to have a permanent basis on which to act, it needs more specific guidance. Other Christian ethicists would simply have us ask, "What would Jesus do?" Others make no major distinctions between Christian and philosophical ethics and simply urge us to do the right thing.

I think, however, that when we hear the call to follow Christ, we are Word-empowered and Spirit-led to walk the way of the Son—the way of filiation—with God. I am not saying with Jon Sobrino that the way of the Son is our way *to* God. I am saying it is our way *with* God. To know Christ is to follow him. As we respond to the call "Follow me," we learn more about the one who calls us, more about the one who is called (ourselves), and more about the journey we share together in the world (our evangelistic outreach).

The Scripture describes the way of filiation as (1) the way of incarnation, (2) the way of the cross, and (3) the way of resurrection. In all spheres of life, both as individual Christians and as the church, we are empowered by the Word and led by the Spirit to walk this way as we respond to the call.

The Way of Incarnation

God's way into the world through Jesus Christ is the way of suffering with the poor and marginalized of society. God's choosing the son of a poor carpenter from obscure Nazareth is not accidental; it is the lens through which God chose to look at our human society and thus to empower the poor and the oppressed. This is also the way through which the Spirit has led God's people throughout the ages, not triumphalism but only servanthood. Only as we look at the world through the eyes of the poor, the homeless, and the politically powerless, do we see the world as Christ sees it and thus understand why we are sent into the world.

We are empowered by the Word and led by the Spirit to walk the way of incarnation, in which we express our liberation as we empower the poor and the voiceless to effect their own liberation. This is the breaking forth of the power that God's creative Word bestows on us.

The Way of the Cross

The way of the cross is Jesus' way of offering the self as the instrument of God's righteousness. It is a means of protest. Through the cross Jesus denounces the ways of sinful humanity and takes a stand against inhuman situations in spite of repressions. The cross, therefore, is both a sacrificial willingness to accept the cost of standing with and for the victims of injustice, and also a firm resolution not to allow injustice to have the last word. The way of the cross goes against the grain. It swims against the tide, continually seeking to expose the unjust and violent structures that cause human degradation.

Throughout the history of the church, the Spirit has led God's nomadic people to follow the way of the cross. The way of the cross, however, should not be confused with talk about the cross or even with a theology of the cross, which, as Gerhard Forde says, "puts roses on the cross." It means a cruciform life of obedience to the leading of the Spirit, liberating us from the work of the flesh so that we can be free for the care of others (Gal. 5:16–25).

The way of incarnation leads the church into the way of the cross, for as the church takes its stand with the impoverished masses, bringing them hope for their liberation, it will certainly be crucified by those who profit from the oppression of the poor. This is our present experience in Madagascar. Since the churches came together and dared to uncover the corruption and crimes of the powers that be and to stand with the people in their call for structural reform, the churches have become the target of repression and severe criticism.

The way of incarnation leading into the way of the cross is also the way of all evangelistic outreach performed by individual Christians. Where racial prejudice, for instance, is allowed to prevail, a Christian's stand with a victim of such prejudice will bring repression on that Christian even from within his/her own family.

The Way of Resurrection

The way of resurrection is Jesus' way of liberating empowerment. As Jesus Christ conquered death and has the final word over death, no death-dealing powers or structures bear the character of necessity or finality. The way of resurrection challenges them all as the Spirit leads the church into the world to proclaim the triumph of resurrection life through direct, transformative, and liberating actions. The way of resurrection makes a way out of no way. With the leading of the Spirit, the way of resurrection transforms every human dead-end into a starting point for the people of God; every social problem into an opportunity; every political crisis into a new beginning.

Lutheranism: Confessional or Confessing?

JUSTIFICATION BY GRACE RECEIVED THROUGH FAITH, AS WE HAVE already explained, points not only to our gracious reception by God but also to the purpose of our being in the world, namely, our gracious sending by God. "You did not choose me, but I chose you and appointed you that you should go and bear fruit" (John 15:16). To be faithful to this justification by grace is to be for the world, to engage in evangelical outreach in all spheres of life: the family, the society, the economy, the state. It is to walk the way of filiation.

The Lutheran church is a Confessional and a confessing church. It acts out what it believes, namely, that God is empowering it through Word and Sacraments to proclaim the good news of Jesus Christ to the world in word and deed. Faith-ing the *sola fide* is following Christ through the way of the Son. It is as we walk this way of filiation that we prophesy to the world. That is, we bring our future with God into our present with God. To walk the way of filiation is the prophethood of all believers. Through this ministry of prophecy, which is the ministry of Word and Sacraments, the Word that has created the sacramental self continues to create and transform the face of the earth. As we follow Christ, we no longer indulge in a ministry of priestly remembrance for the sake of the frightened conscience, but rather we engage in a ministry of empowering prophethood for the sake of the weak and the impoverished of the land.